THE BLUE AND WHITE ROAD

A PATH TO A FULFILLING JEWISH LIFE

RABBI MICHAEL C. SIMON

Published in the United States by CreateSpace

ISBN: 1477452516
ISBN 13: 9781477452516

Cover Photograph by Deborah Rubin

As Jews, our obligation is not just to simply believe. Rather, like our Patriarch Jacob, our obligation is to wrestle, struggle, and engage with both God and man.

Praise for the Blue and White Road

"Rabbi Michael Simon's THE BLUE AND WHITE ROAD: A Path to a Fulfilling Jewish Life offers a treasure of wise insights pertaining to all aspects of modern Jewish life. I enjoyed his humor and wisdom. This is a book for all Jews to read and savor!"

Rabbi Michael Leo Samuel, Temple Beth Shalom, Chula Vista, California;
Author, Birth and Rebirth Through Genesis: The Timeless Theological Conversation

"Rabbi Simon has a wonderful talent of putting Torah teachings into everyday language that allows the reader to say-"Yes! I can do that!" Enjoyable, must reading for all who are searching for ways to be Jewish in modern times like ours!"

Rabbi Bertram Kieffer, Sunrise Jewish Center, Sunrise, Florida

TABLE OF CONTENTS

Acknowledgements xiii

Foreword xv

PART I – A JEWISH IDENTITY
  Chapter 1 – A Return To Judaism 3
  Chapter 2 – Looking Both Ways 7
  Chapter 3 – Kosher Enough? 11
  Chapter 4 – Grasshoppers And Giants 15
  Chapter 5 – If You Will It, It Is No Dream 19
  Chapter 6 – Inter–Marriage 25
  Chapter 7 – How To Be Jewish 31
  Chapter 8 – The Bush Still Burns 37

PART II – GROWING CLOSER TO GOD
  Chapter 1 – God's Voice 43
  Chapter 2 – Voices of Torah 47
  Chapter 3 – Where Is God? 51
  Chapter 4 – Altars And Synagogues 55
  Chapter 5 – Prayer 61
  Chapter 6 – Sixth Sense 65
  Chapter 7 – A Hanukkah Message 71
  Chapter 6 – Tebowing 77
  Chapter 8 – Knowing God 83

PART III – HERITAGE AND TRADITION

Chapter 1 – Faith and Chesed 91

Chapter 2 – Stairway To Heaven 95

Chapter 3 – Angels 101

Chapter 4 – And Demons 105

Chapter 5 – No Jew Left Behind 109

Chapter 6 – Speak Loudly And Carry A Big Stick 113

Chapter 7 – Bringing The Mashiach 119

Chapter 8 – What Is Hanukkah 123

Chapter 9 – Heroes and Villains 129

PART IV – ETHICS AND VALUES

Chapter 1 – Spirit 135

Chapter 2 – Priceless 141

Chapter 3 – One Small Step For Man 147

Chapter 4 – Request, Not Demand 153

Chapter 5 – Selflessness 157

Chapter 6 – Winning Isn't Everything 161

Chapter 7 – SHH! – Simple, Haimish And Humble ... 165

Chapter 8 – The Perfect Game 171

Chapter 9 – Israel's Values 177

PART V – COMMUNITY AND CIVILITY

Chapter 1 – The Best of Times; The Worst of Times ... 185

Chapter 2 – Ahavat Yisrael 191

Chapter 3 – Who Decides? 195

Chapter 4 – Christmas 199

Chapter 5 – Inauguration 205

Chapter 6 – A Visit To Church 209

Chapter 7 – Make Me A Sanctuary 215
Chapter 8 – A Decade After 9/11 221

PART VI – LIFE–LONG LEARNING
Chapter 1 – Positive Judaism 227
Chapter 2 – Shemitism 233
Chapter 3 – Fifteen Minutes of Wisdom 237
Chapter 4 – EdJEWcation 241
Chapter 5 – The Four Sons In The 21st Century 245
Chapter 6 – A Daily Seder 251
Chapter 7 – A Two Minute Elevator Ride 255

PART VII – A FULFILLING JEWISH LIFE
Chapter 1 – Having A Vision 261
Chapter 2 – Circles 265
Chapter 3 – Israel at Sixty–Four 269
Chapter 4 – EvanJEWlical 275
Chapter 5 – A Baseball Yizkor 281
Chapter 6 – Finishing Our Books 287
Chapter 7 – Follow The Blue And White Road 291

In Conclusion – May The Lord 301

ACKNOWLEDGEMENTS

I would like to acknowledge a number of people who have not only encouraged me to write this book, but who have encouraged and supported me on my own life's path.

My Rabbis and teachers, too numerous to name individually, who I've learned much from over the years, especially Moshe Ezry, who enabled me to do more than I ever thought I was capable of doing.

In these pages I often say that Judaism is an adult religion. Steven A. Solomon first showed me this when he hired me to teach Hebrew School many years ago and fostered my appreciation for Judaism as an adult. I'd like to thank him for his friendship and guidance over the years.

My many students, past and present, young and old alike, in a variety of settings and places, have inspired me and have helped shape my own thoughts about Judaism; much of which is represented on these pages.

I would be remiss if I didn't acknowledge some special people in my life; my mother-in-law Louise Licht, my brother Richard and his family, Michael Brooker, Channa Chanover, Jules Frankel, Simeon and Sophie Gottlieb, Iva, Brad, Rose, Marcy and Katie Morris, and Mickey Seide. I wouldn't be in a position to write this book if it wasn't for their continuous friendship and encouragement.

Deborah Rubin, Robert Rubin, Esq., Liz Harris, and Connie Hall reviewed all or parts of my manuscript. I am indebted to them for taking the time to do so and offering their invaluable advice, suggestions and insight. Deborah Rubin is also responsible for taking the photo of me on the back cover and she spent countless hours getting it just right.

Of course this book would not be possible without the constant support, love, and respect shown to me by my congregants at Temple Beth Kodesh, a very special place, filled with incredibly special people.

And to my children, Samantha and Jason, whom I love, who inspire me, who make me proud every day to be their father, and to whom I entrust this legacy.

Last but not least, my beloved wife Andrea, who's love, support, patience, and understanding, is unending, and I am forever grateful. Andrea insisted that I dedicate this book to my parents, z"l. But I'm sure my parents would agree with me that this book deserves to be dedicated to her, and so I do.

FOREWORD

A number of years ago I was talking with Bob Rosenthal, the then President of Temple Beth Kodesh, about the shul, about future plans, programs, and ideas, etc. It's what rabbis and shul presidents spend a lot of time doing. In the course of this conversation Bob said, "Rabbi, you should write a book." So Bob, I took your advice. I wrote a book!

I hope this book serves as a catalyst in making Judaism meaningful and relevant for Jews living in the twenty-first century. As you read through the pages that follow, I hope it encourages you to live as a more active, involved, and knowledgeable Jew, and to make Judaism an important and central part of your life.

Let me begin with this thought. Many of us have different ideas about what a Jew is. In no particular order, and by no means exhaustive, here is my definition.

A Jew is someone who supports Israel; a Jew is someone who supports the Jewish community by belonging to a synagogue; a Jew is someone who helps make a minyan so that those who are saying kaddish can do so; a Jew is someone who visits the sick; a Jew is someone who is proud of his heritage; a Jew is someone who engages in tikkun olam, repairing the world; a Jew is someone who cares about the less fortunate; a Jew is someone who not only gives, but does, tzedakah; a Jew is someone who knows that his purpose in life involves more than just his own self interests; a Jew is someone who learns and studies; a Jew is someone who raises Jewish children; a Jew is someone who expresses his gratitude to God on a regular basis. A Jew is someone who can even completely ignore this list or only select one or two definitions, or come up with his or her own list, and still be considered Jewish.

Finally, a Jew is someone who adheres to the statement made by Ruth, a convert, and the great-grandmother of King David, who famously replied to her mother-in-law Naomi, "Your people will be my people, and your God will be my God."

To paraphrase the words of the great sage Hillel, "The rest of the book is commentary. Now go and read!"

PART I
A JEWISH IDENTITY

A RETURN TO JUDAISM 1

O ne of our favorite Jewish foods, although not so uniquely Jewish anymore, is the bagel. Of course, when it comes to the bagel, the question that is always asked is, "Why is there a hole in the middle of the bagel?" My answer is that the hole exists to remind us, whenever we eat our morning bagel, that we have a hole in our Jewish lives. And it is our task and our responsibility to fill that hole; to fill it with a Jewish life; with Jewish pride; with Jewish learning; and with Jewish culture.

Another aspect of the bagel is its circular shape; a shape which has no beginning nor end. While we refer to the idea of coming full circle, the truth is, that as Jews, we have yet to come full circle. We have yet to return to that place where both we and the bagel were, are, and will continue to be, uniquely Jewish. To use a familiar term which resonates during the High Holiday season, we have yet to do "Teshuvah." We have yet to come full circle as Jews and we have yet to fill that hole in our lives with Judaism.

At its root, teshuvah literally means return; a return to our Jewish roots and heritage. It is a recognition that although we may have strayed, the door is always open for our return. We hope and pray that our return will be with greater vigor and a commitment which lasts for the rest of our lives, which impacts and affects our lives, and not just lasts for a few hours or days.

People stray from Judaism for a variety of reasons. It might have been because of an experience which turned them off to Judaism, perhaps an anti-Semitic experience, or perhaps being forced by our parents to go to shul or to Hebrew School. And while there, maybe we couldn't understand what we were taught, like how God could make Abraham sacrifice his son Isaac. Maybe it involved seeing Judaism as a rigid set of dos and don'ts, while at the same time not seeing and appreciating the true essence and beauty of Judaism. It might even have been a tragic event, like the loss of a loved one, which caused us to lose faith in God.

If any of these experiences apply to you, or even if you've had different experiences, we always have the chance, every day, to re-examine these issues, to confront them head on, to erase our doubts, to strengthen our faith, and to get closer to God.

The essence of Judaism however, is that despite straying, everyone has the opportunity to return and to reclaim a missing piece of their Jewish identity. We never know what might bring us back. We never know what event in our lives will cause us to return, which is why we need to be open to the possibility that some such event might in fact occur.

The best illustration of our ability to return is the life story of the famous actor Kirk Douglas. For reasons many of us can relate to, Douglas strayed from the Judaism of his childhood as he grew older. However, at the age of seventy five, he was involved in a helicopter crash which killed two people. Douglas woke up in the hospital tormented by guilt over having survived that crash, and questioning why he was still alive while two young people died. He searched for answers and eventually found the answers he was looking for in a place he never thought would be possible; in Judaism.

Then, during a trip to Israel, Douglas finally managed to overcome his childhood understanding of Judaism, his fears and doubts about Judaism, and began to see and appreciate Judaism for what it truly is. Kirk Douglas came to a realization we should all take to heart. As he said, "It has been pointed out to me that no rational adult would make a business decision based on what they knew when they were thirteen. You wouldn't decide who to marry based on what you knew about love and relationships when you were thirteen. But lots of us seem satisfied to dismiss religion based on what we learned at thirteen, and I was one of those that stupid."

Kirk Douglas teaches us that it's never too late to return, and that it's never too late to learn more, to study more, and to become more involved. He also points out the glaring truth that Judaism should not just be seen through the eyes of a child, but that as adults we can come to truly understand its essence and meaning.

Let's not wait for our own helicopter crash to return to God, to work through our fears and doubts about Judaism and about God, and to reinvigorate our Jewish identities. Instead we can seek answers to our questions, if only we take the time to ask.

Let us also understand that our opinions and view of Judaism can be seen through our experiences as adults, and not through our fears as a child. We should therefore listen to that voice in the background, like the angel over Abraham's shoulder as he was about to sacrifice his son Isaac, telling us to stop what we are doing and to come back; because it's never too late to return.

LOOKING BOTH WAYS 2

T he events which took place in the beginning of the Book of Exodus are so familiar that they don't need to be recounted here. However, of all these events, including the burning bush, the ten plagues, the Exodus, the crossing of the Red Sea, the receiving of the Ten Commandments on Mount Sinai, a strong argument can be made that the most important event to happen to the Jewish people (at least in the Torah) was when Moses struck and killed the Egyptian taskmaster.

The Torah, in its usually brief form, says the following: "And it happened in those days that Moses grew up and went out to his brothers and saw their burdens. And he saw an Egyptian man striking a Hebrew man, from his brothers. He turned this way and that and saw there was no man, so he struck down the Egyptian and hid him in the sand."

Moses knew the Israelite slaves were his brothers because, as the Midrash tells us, when Pharaoh's daughter rescued Moses, she brought his mother and sister as nurses for him.

Accepting this Midrash at face value, it's entirely possible that Moses knew all along he was not really Egyptian. Having been raised in Egyptian royalty Moses probably didn't really care or think about his Jewish background. He was very happy with the privileged life he had and he gave no thought whatsoever to the sufferings and plight of the Hebrew slaves.

Until... until he happened to go out to where the Israelites were working and he saw something. He saw the Egyptian taskmaster beating the Hebrew slave, one of his brothers. This outraged Moses. Maybe it was because of the injustice of the treatment of the Hebrews. Or maybe it was because the slave being beaten wasn't just a slave, but was one of his brothers!

Seeing one of your brothers, or a family member, or a friend being harmed is more likely to evoke a stronger response from a person than watching a stranger be harmed. It hits closer to home. Now, maybe for the first time, Moses realized his connection to the Jewish people. So he acted. He acted harshly. He killed the taskmaster. But not before something else occurred. "He turned this way and that."

Why did Moses turn "this way and that?" What was he looking for? Did he want to make sure no one else was watching? Or was it something else; something that describes Moses' inner struggle; the struggle between his Jewish side and his Egyptian side? Moses realized a choice must be made. Who was he? Was he an Egyptian or was he a Jew?

When Moses saw the Egyptian strike the Hebrew slave, he realized that he could no longer remain neutral. He also realized there was nobody around who could help him. He either had to accept his Egyptian culture with its treatment of the Jews, or he had to do something about it. Moses decided to kill the Egyptian and bury him in the sand, and with it, to symbolically bury that part of his life, the Egyptian part. From then on, his allegiance and affiliation were with the Jewish people.

The rabbinic commentators portray this incident as a turning point in the development of Moses as a leader of the Jewish people and in the development of the Jewish people themselves. Moses could have done nothing. That would have been in the best interests of his family, the Egyptian family. Instead he looked around. Moses saw his family on the one side and his people on the other, and he chose.....his people.

Understanding the common good is one reason why God chose Moses. He saw in Moses the essential character trait needed to be the person to lead the Jews out of Egypt and give them the Torah. God saw that Moses understood the concept of peoplehood and He saw that Moses was willing to sacrifice personal family happiness and quality family time in order to be the leader of the people. Not everyone is able or willing to do that; to sacrifice themselves, their egos, their grand designs, for the good of the whole; for the betterment of the whole community. That is fine. Not everyone can be like Moses. Not everyone can be a "leader".

There is another explanation for Moses' looking "this way and that" which doesn't only apply to him as a leader, but is something that can apply to each and every one of us. Moses looked "this way and that" and what did he see? He saw the life of a Jew on the one side and he saw a secular life on the other. Back then the two were diametrically opposed. Moses saw the conflict between choosing the secular life of the surrounding culture and choosing a life of Jewish identity.

Moses was the first to resolve this conflict which would only later become more acute for us.

Too many Jews today look this way and that way and choose "that way." They choose the life of the secular culture. They don't choose to live a Jewish life. They don't choose to be part of a people. After all, the other side is so much more enticing and so much easier. Today, when the lines are so blurred between this way and that way, many people don't even realize which way they are looking. They only see one path - the path of assimilation.

This is why Moses' behavior is so important and relevant to us. Not just because he exercised leadership skills, but because he realized there was a clear Jewish life which could be led, and a separate and distinct Jewish identity which could be had.

The Jewish way does not only have to be a 100% Shomer Shabbat, strictly observant way. But as Moses realized, there is always a separate and distinct Jewish identity. We can never lose this identity, for if we do, we are doomed to extinction.

When we reach certain crossroads in our lives, when we come across decisions that have to be made, remember to also look this way and that. Remember to look for our Jewish identity. Remember to ask "What would Moses do?" "What would God want us to do?" "What is in my best interests as a Jew or for the Jewish community to do?" There can be many correct ways of answering these questions. The only wrong answer is to not ask the question in the first place and to not look both ways.

KOSHER ENOUGH? 3

Other than by being born Jewish or converting to Judaism, are there any outward signs that makes a person Jewish? If someone met us for the first time, how would they know we were Jewish? One can't even say it's when we tell them our name because it's not that uncommon today to find a Goldberg who is a Catholic and a Duffy who is Jewish. Since we really don't have horns, the answer cannot be, when they ask to see the horns. So what makes us Jewish? For me it's easy. When people see my kippah they know, or should know, that I'm Jewish.

There is however one outward sign, one aspect to our behavior and actions which will let others know that we are Jewish. That sign is the observance of Kashrut. Even though the Torah never uses that term, keeping kosher, eating only what the Torah allows, is certainly one way, if not the foremost way, of letting another person know that we're Jewish.

If there is one behavior or belief which separates Jews from non-Jews, it's the laws of Kashrut. Christians have a

11

Sabbath - its Sunday. Muslims don't eat pork- only Hallal meat. But they don't have the rest of our kashrut laws.

If we were to ask a non-Jew what makes Jews different - not for any stereotypical or anti-Semitic reason- but in general what makes us different, keeping kosher, not eating pork or bacon, or lobster or shrimp, would surely stand out as one of the top reasons, if not the number one reason why we are different. This is why kashrut is so important to Judaism.

The laws of kashrut are so involved and detailed that they are enough to turn people off. The laws of kashrut can get so bogged down in minutiae that we lose sight of their original purpose; to remind us, each and every time we eat, that we should recognize our Jewish identity and recognize that we must eat differently because of that.

If we go to a restaurant and we tell our dining companion that the reason why we're not ordering the lobster special is because we're kosher, we've expressed our Jewish identity. We've stood up and made a statement that we're Jewish. If we go to a friend's house for a Bar-B-Q and don't eat the cheeseburger because it's not kosher, we've expressed our Jewish identity. We've reminded ourselves as well as our friends that we are Jewish. We've reminded ourselves and told our friends that we are not only Jewish when we come to shul and we are not only Jewish when we are praying, but that we are Jewish outside as well. We carry our Jewish identity card with us wherever we go and we take it out as our own personal dinner menu.

Many people don't keep kosher because they feel it's an all or nothing proposition. It's not! But we should at least be on the kashrut ladder. We should at least have some limitation on our food habits because it's a way of maintaining our Jewish identity.

Where does one start? Start by not eating pork or shellfish. When we see them on a menu, and we don't order them for no other reason other than because they're not kosher, we are making a powerful statement about our own Jewish identity. Yes I'm Jewish. I might not be a perfect Jew, but here is a way, a very public way, that I can express my Jewish identity. Understand also that most people, non-Jews especially, are very respectful of the fact that we cannot or will not eat certain foods because they are not kosher. I know from first-hand experience that people are willing to be quite accommodating out of respect for the fact that we are so respectful of our religion and identity.

It is easier to keep kosher today due to the numerous kosher products on the market. So let us recognize that keeping kosher, on some level at least, is an important part of our Jewish identity because it continually lets others know that we are Jewish. No matter our personal kashrut standards, levels or habits, raising our kashrut observance serves to increase our Jewish identity. And we must always be proud of, and public with, our Jewish identity.

Grasshoppers And Giants

4

Many Jewish jokes, and there are countless ones out there, poke fun at ourselves. They call attention to our foibles, insecurities and weaknesses. Even when the Jew emerges as the winner, it's still at a cost. It still pokes fun at us. Because of our history, we tend to go along with these jokes and stories and laugh at them. However, these jokes, and similar humorous stories, have served though to create an image of the Jew which has not always been for the best. Perhaps over time, listening to these jokes has had the effect of creating a rather low Jewish self-image or Jewish self esteem. We tend to believe these stories about ourselves. We therefore get bogged down in these stereotypes and not see our way out of them.

Unfortunately, this low self-esteem didn't come about because of bad or stereotypical jokes. It began when Moses sent out twelve spies to scout out the Land of Canaan. After scouting the land for forty days the spies came back and reported that there were giants living in there. They said, "We saw ourselves as grasshoppers, and that's what they thought of us, too." Herein lies the problem. It was bad enough that the spies thought of themselves as grasshoppers. But how could they possibly have known that the inhabitants of Canaan thought of them as grasshoppers also?

They couldn't know for sure. However, because they had such low self esteem, so little confidence in their own abilities and the justness of their cause, they not only saw themselves as small and as insignificant as a grasshopper, but they also projected that view into the eyes of the Canaanites. In other words, because the spies saw themselves as being so low, so unworthy, it was only natural for them to believe that others would see them that way too, even if there was no evidence of it. That was the beginning of low Jewish self esteem.

Do we still think of ourselves as grasshoppers? Unfortunately the answer is yes. Do we still think that others see us as grasshoppers? Again, unfortunately the answer is yes. So long as we continue to see ourselves as grasshoppers, then so will others, and they will take advantage. Jewish self esteem, Jewish self image, has been battered for centuries and it continues to take a beating today.

Let me share with you this example from a sermon I once gave on the Middle East. I wrote in part, "And now is not the time to be constantly worrying about the reaction of the rest of the world. Israel will be criticized and vilified no matter what." That sermon was forwarded to a person living in Israel, who e-mailed me the following:

"I'm afraid that we can't afford to let our relationship with the US get cold and be isolated from the rest of the world. Maybe that is because I come from the 'galut' and I still worry 'what the goyim will think'. But we must at least act conciliatory and let the Palestinians turn down peace offers! Why show the world a stubborn face? As our late lamented Teddy Roosevelt said 'Speak softly and carry a big stick." Netanyahu should address himself to the world, not to the right wing at home."

That e-mail was written by someone who is always worried about how everyone else perceives us and by someone who thinks and acts like a grasshopper. The truth is that it is only by acting like giants can we truly be giants. In 1948 Israel was surrounded by five Arab armies who were larger and better equipped, and intent on her destruction. Israel had one pistol for every ten soldiers. But in the Israelis' own eyes, they were invincible. They were giants, not grasshoppers. Because they had that self image, they were. Because they had that self-image, they were victorious. Because Israel still maintains that self-image today, no longer should we ever again see ourselves as grasshoppers. No longer should we ever again for a moment believe that others see us that way either.

The spies should never have said that they were looked at by others as grasshoppers, because it should never bother us how another person views us. The person who constantly worries about how others view him will have no peace. If it takes the approval of others to give you self-worth, you will never feel good about yourself.

We can all achieve spiritual greatness if we try, if we persevere, and if we believe. We can all do it regardless of our physical stature or condition. As a Jew, never see yourself as a grasshopper, but rather as one of the "anakim," one of the giants. Have a strong sense of self, a sense of worth and a strong sense of Jewish values. Don't waste your time worrying that others might think of you as a grasshopper because, for all you know, in their eyes, you might truly be a giant! In that case, don't you owe it to yourself, don't you owe it to your family and friends, don't you owe it to your community, don't you owe it to the Jewish people, to truly be a giant?

IF YOU WILL IT, IT IS NO DREAM   5

Whenever the Ten Commandments are read publicly from the Torah we stand in order to symbolically re-create the experience of being at Mount Sinai 3,500 years ago. That is also why Moses repeated the Ten Commandments in the Book of Deuteronomy. He wanted the new generation to experience what it must have been like forty years earlier. He repeated the surrounding experience. He painted a picture of how the sky darkened, how there was thunder and lightning, how a voice came out of the darkness, how the mountain was ablaze with fire, how the people trembled before the presence of God. He impressed upon the people of that later generation that they all experienced this tremendous event together and survived.

Maybe we can learn something from Moses. More important than the rules and laws is the experience. In order to impress upon us the importance of Judaism and our tradition, we can't just teach it but we have to experience it. Yes, we can learn by rote, and we can learn laws and learn a trade, but the best way of learning is by experiencing.

The experiences that we have as Jews must be meaningful, relevant and age appropriate. Today, perhaps more than ever, it is important to build a positive Jewish identity among our children. If we share Jewish experiences, repeat them and find joy and meaning in them, the rest will follow. Don't worry; you have the rest of your lives to learn the laws and rituals and history.

Unfortunately, it's not as easy as it sounds. Sometimes we get so caught up in our own lives that we neglect these experiences until it's too late. Then we bemoan the consequences. However a court case from a few years ago shows us that even if it's too late to share the experiences, it's never too late to foster a Jewish identity and impress our will and our values on our descendants.

An Illinois couple actually put a provision in their Last Will and Testaments that their grandchildren can inherit $250,000 each but only if they either marry a Jew or the person converts within one year of marriage. Coercion? Yes. But so what. Coercion from God doesn't work anymore. Maybe financial coercion will.

This couple decided to make a statement. They decided that it was important to them that their grandchildren marry a member of the Jewish faith and carry on their traditions and experiences and pass them down to their great-grandchildren. Like Moses, they could have just sat down and explained to their grandchildren the Jewish prohibition on inter-marriage. Would it have been effective? Would it have had any impact?

I don't know. I don't know the family. Maybe they could have tried to use some guilt.

They decided to be like Moses and make their grandchildren sit up and take notice. Moses did it by relating his experience. This couple did it by relating their money. In essence, they put their money where their mouths were. They said, nothing else works. Nothing else matters to you. So let us put it in terms you can understand. Marrying a Jew is important to us. So if you carry out our wishes you will be handsomely rewarded. If not, well...........

As it turned out, only one of this couple's five grandchildren married a Jewish spouse and stood to inherit. The others sued their own grandparents to declare the Will invalid and to get the money. Who cares about the grandparents' wishes? We just want the money, not the tradition or experience that comes with it. And that is truly sad.

The Illinois trial court hearing the case then declared it illegal as against public policy to state in a person's Last Will and Testament that if one's grandchildren do not marry a spouse of the Jewish faith, it is as if they were dead and ineligible to inherit. An appeals court however overturned that decision and re-instated the Will.

In the end, no matter how the courts ruled, these grandparents took a stand and relayed not only to their grandchildren, but to all of us as well, what is really important. They wanted their great-grandchildren to have certain experiences. They wanted their great-grandchildren to be able to stand at Mount Sinai as their ancestors once did. They wanted their great-grandchildren to experience Jewish tradition and history, perhaps just as they did.

These wishes were then expressed in no uncertain terms, in the best way they knew how; by attaching a financial incentive to their wishes. As it turned out, not only did their grandchildren take notice, but many more as well. Ultimately, their wishes might not be carried out, but only because their grandchildren were more concerned with money than with Jewish tradition. It will be on these grandchildren's consciences that they sued their grandparents to get their hands on the money rather than respecting their grandparents' wishes.

A part of the court's opinion reinstating the Will bears repeating because it speaks of the importance of Jewish identity and experience and is expressed in a way that could easily be written by a rabbi or by anyone else who understands the importance of this issue to the Jewish community.

"[His] intent was to benefit those descendants who opted to honor and further his commitment to Judaism by marrying within the faith. He had expressed his concern about the potential extinction of the Jewish people, not only by holocaust, but by gradual dilution as a result of intermarriage with non-Jews. A grandparent in his situation is entirely free during his lifetime to attempt to influence his grandchildren to marry within his family's religious tradition, even by offering financial incentives to do so."

The court goes on to say, "Equal protection does not require that all children be treated equally;... and the free exercise clause does not require a grandparent to treat grandchildren who reject his religious beliefs and customs in the same manner as he treats those who conform to his traditions."

This case presents an unfortunate turn of events any way we look at it, and there's probably a lot more going on here than meets the eye. However, there's a lesson here for all of us. Despite the legalities, our Last Will and Testament is our final opportunity to relate our experiences, our Jewish identity, and our hopes for our children and grandchildren. We should share with them our experiences. Yes, we should do it while we're alive, but even if we don't, we still have the ability to do so even after we're gone. Like these grandparents realized, perhaps a little too late, Jewish identity, Jewish experience, and Jewish continuity, are truly important.

Inter-Marriage 6

A few years ago Chelsea Clinton, the daughter of former President Bill Clinton and Secretary of State Hillary Clinton, who is a Methodist, married Mark Mezvinsky, a Jew. This wedding was officiated by Reverend William Shillady, a Methodist minister, and by Rabbi James Ponet, a Reform Rabbi, who serves as the director of Yale University's Slifka Center for Jewish Life. Mr. Mezvinsky wore a kippah and a tallit, they stood under a chuppah, there was a ketubah, friends recited the sheva brachot, and Mr. Mezvinsky stepped on a glass at the conclusion of the ceremony. Other than the fact that this wedding took place on Shabbat, there was a Methodist minister officiating, and the bride wasn't Jewish, it sounds like a typical Jewish wedding.

Our reaction to this wedding? WOW, look how far we've come! The daughter of a President of the United States marries a Jewish man and nobody bats an eyelash. It makes us stop and ask, what's the big deal about inter-marriage anyway? Why do we oppose it so strenuously?

The primary answer to our opposition to inter-marriage is based on the fear that intermarriage will destroy the Jewish people. Unfortunately, for those who inter-marry because they have no connection to Judaism, that fear, that concern, is irrelevant. Those who inter-marry but still care about Judaism look to Mark Mezvinsky and say, "See, I can inter-marry and still care and still pass my traditions to my children. So you see. Don't worry. Intermarriage won't be the end the Jewish people."

If our main reason, fear, is no longer an effective deterrent to inter-marriage, we must then blame ourselves. We failed. We can't blame the Mezvinskys of the world for our failings. One commentator on this wedding blamed the Jewish people as a whole for not giving him the experience and knowledge that he needed to be proud to be a Jew and to fight the temptation of inter-marriage.

The problem however isn't that we failed. The problem isn't that Mr. Mezvinsky has no Jewish pride. The problem isn't that Mr. Mezvinsky has no Jewish knowledge. The problem isn't that Mr. Mezvinsky didn't go to Hebrew School, or visit a Sukkah, or have a Shabbat dinner. Many Jews with significant Jewish backgrounds marry outside the faith. I even know of classmates from Yeshivah who are inter-married.

No. The "problem" is that even to people who still want to be Jewish, marrying a non-Jew is not seen as any cause for alarm, as anything unusual, anything to be ashamed about, or as anything that will cause everlasting harm to the Jewish people. If we have a failure at all, it is that we have failed to come up with valid, meaningful, and relevant reasons why it's important to marry someone who is Jewish. We have failed to come up with a way of convincing an intelligent, identifiable Jew, who is nonetheless proud of his or her heritage, why today, in the twenty-first century, marrying a fellow Jew is still so very important. Maybe though, there is an answer.

One night my son was making a corned beef and pastrami sandwich for dinner. Since he doesn't like mustard, he put.... mayonnaise on the sandwich. "Uch," I said. "How goyish."

My son looked at me like I was nuts. After all, what's the big deal about mayonnaise and corned beef? I guess he didn't get it. I mean how un-Jewish can that be? Mayonnaise on corned beef? We might understand; but he is of a different generation.

Then my son hit on what is to me the crux of the inter-marriage problem. Sensing my utter disappointment over his condiment preference, he turned to me and said, "I must really be a true disappointment to the Jewish people." Not to his parents, mind you, but to the Jewish people! He recognized his responsibility to the Jewish people as a whole to live (ok, eat) a certain way. It is that sense of responsibility to the Jewish people that is missing from the whole inter-marriage debate.

The issue isn't that an individual can't marry a non-Jewish spouse and still remain Jewish, be proud of his or her heritage as a Jew or still want to be part of the Jewish community. The problem is that we live in our twenty-first century enlightened society where we constantly mix and mingle with people from a variety of cultures and backgrounds. The problem is that religion and religious differences don't separate us as they once did because we are more tolerant of other religions and cultures and lifestyles than ever before. Given the above, isn't it fair to say that in this age and culture, Jewish "people-hood" is not a concept or an ideal many young Jews of marriageable age believe is important?

Furthermore, the problem is that we no longer live in the ghetto, or the shtetl, or the neighborhood, where we are only surrounded by our fellow Jews. We want our children to succeed in this world, so we send them to the best colleges, and we send them into the non-Jewish world to work. Look at our success in doing so! However at the same time, it's led to the high rates of inter-marriage.

When we're out in the larger non-Jewish world, we run the high risk of meeting and falling in love with someone of a different faith. The prevailing attitude is Jewish, Catholic, Methodist, or Buddhist; it doesn't matter. We're all God's children. We all get along. So what if we do things a little differently. It's okay as long as we respect each other's beliefs and differences and learn from them. The idea of belonging to a separate people, a main reason advanced all these years for the prohibition on inter-marriage, is a foreign concept in today's world. That is why the wedding section of the New York Times contains countless numbers of not only interfaith, but inter-racial and inter-cultural marriages which are so prevalent today.

And so we have a choice. We can either come up with a better reason for being against inter-marriage than the idea of peoplehood, or we can do a better job of explaining why peoplehood is such an important concept to our Jewish identity; why we can't have a Jewish religion without a Jewish people.

If we are serious about combating inter-marriage, we must do a better job of giving our enlightened, educated, and multi-cultural society living youngsters, a reason, a good reason, a new reason, and a sensible reason, for not marrying outside the faith. In other words, we must not only stress and reinforce the idea of peoplehood, but also make that idea relevant, meaningful and important to a Jew in the twenty-first century.

The bottom line is that we must instill better Jewish values and a better sense of identity among our Jewish children. We must find better ways of kiruv, of bringing inter-married families into our Jewish community. And most importantly, we must encourage inter-faith families to raise their children as Jews, with a strong sense of Jewish identity.

How To Be Jewish

7

While "Why be Jewish" is a question seemingly asked over and over again by young and old alike today, the question we really should be asking ourselves, is "How to Be Jewish." This is because the vast majority of Jews today, especially in America, no longer know how to, living as we do in such an assimilated society.

How does one be Jewish today? There are many answers and many ways of doing so, starting with the premise that to be Jewish, we must internalize our Jewish identities. We must understand that Judaism is not something we pick and choose to do whenever we feel like it. It can't only be at brises, bar mitzvahs, weddings, funerals, or other life cycle events.

Once we've internalized our feelings and our identities, once we've recognized the importance of Judaism to our lives, the next step is to become more engaged by doing something a little more Jewish. Suppose one eats a bagel on Sunday morning because that is his or her connection to Judaism. We should encourage that person to then eat chicken for dinner on Friday night in addition to his bagel on Sunday morning.

If we make it a habit of eating chicken on Friday night, then maybe we can make it a habit of eating chicken at home. Maybe we'll make a habit of eating that chicken with our family; maybe we'll have some wine with our chicken dinner; maybe we'll make Kiddush over that wine; and maybe we'll even light Shabbat candles. Before we know it we're having a traditional Shabbat dinner.

It sounds easy but more Jews don't do this because they feel that unless they do it all the time they're being hypocrites. If we drive to shul on Shabbat we're hypocrites. If we keep a kosher home but eat non-kosher outside, we're hypocrites. We'd rather do nothing than be a hypocrite. But Judaism is not an all or nothing proposition. We shouldn't have to choose between living in the seventeenth century on the one hand or modernizing Judaism to such a degree that it is unrecognizable on the other.

We should be happy and proud of the Jewish practices we perform because even the bare minimum is infinitely better than nothing. As the metaphor of Jacob's ladder reminds us, one needn't be at the top rung of the ladder to be considered a good Jew. But we should at least be on the ladder and we should at least aim to reach higher and do more.

An easy and important step, is being part of a Jewish community. We must see ourselves not as isolated individuals, but as part of a five thousand year old tradition and community of people, all sharing the same heritage and identity. Whether one is observant or not, one can still be part of that community.

I asked a number of Orthodox friends what draws them to that particular aspect of Judaism. The common thread running through their responses was that in Orthodoxy they find the internalization of their Judaism. They know that they are always Jewish. They know that all aspects of their lives are pervaded by Judaism. They know instinctively that as soon as the shofar sounds on Yom Kippur it doesn't mean see you next year, it means, it's time to build the Sukkah and celebrate the next holiday. Most importantly, they know that they belong to a supportive community.

These answers have absolutely nothing to do with being observant or Shomer Shabbat. They have everything to do with knowledge and pride; identity and community. Even if one does not live a fully observant lifestyle, one can still be authentically Jewish by being part of the Jewish community. What is community? A sense that we are all in this together. "Kol Yisrael Arevim Zeh Lazeh." We just have to make Judaism, Jewish values, and Jewish traditions, an integral part of our lives.

Being part of a supportive community, one of the most appealing aspects of Orthodox Judaism, need not be confined to the Orthodox community. The following examples are actions we all can and must take in order to foster that sense of Jewish identity and Jewish community, to make Judaism not only survive, but thrive.

My dear friend and colleague Rabbi Howard Shub told me how a few years ago he went back home to Toronto to visit his mother at the retirement home in which she lived. Down the street from where he was staying was an Orthodox synagogue where he went on Shabbat. Before he was done, three people, all strangers, invited him to their homes for lunch. The same thing happened to him when he was in New York one Shabbat visiting an Orthodox shul.

At the same time, another friend spent the summer in North Carolina. One Shabbat he visited a Conservative synagogue. The next Shabbat, on Friday night, he went to the Chabad. The Chabad rabbi invited him and his wife over for dinner. It was spur of the moment and unplanned, but there was a guest in the shul and that is how they welcome guests. This is how we can welcome guests as well!

A few years ago I called the Chabad rabbi in my community for help in building my Sukkah. Although we had never formally met, by the end of the conversation I was given a choice. Which night of Sukkot are Andrea and I coming over to his house for dinner! Can there be a nicer way of building friendship, camaraderie and closeness than by going to shul for services and then sharing a Shabbat or Yom Tov meal with a fellow Jew?

In order to foster and enhance our Jewish identities, in order to learn how to be Jewish in today's world, we might begin by making our synagogues, and our community, our second family, especially on Shabbat and holidays. We can make it our business to invite someone over for a Shabbat meal. We don't have to invite everyone over, but invite another person or another couple. It's a mitzvah and since one mitzvah leads to another, hopefully the person we invite will reciprocate. Invite a different congregant the following month, and accept an invitation if one comes your way.

One might be amazed how a simple invitation, can multiply exponentially. It's a way of showing that you can also socialize with the people you pray with. It's a way of showing that our Judaism, our observance of Holidays and traditions does not end with the sounding of the shofar. It's a way of showing that yes, we can be Jewish, we can celebrate our holidays, and at the same time do it in a fun and enjoyable way, while still living in 21st century America!

See someone new in shul? See someone new move into your neighborhood? Invite them over. Don't worry about not having enough food or it not being fancy. The guest will be so touched by the invitation to mind. Most importantly, by doing so, we have taken a step towards not only internalizing our own Judaism but in helping someone else internalize theirs as well. That guest, that visitor, will leave the shul, or leave your home with a better feeling about that place, its people, and about Judaism.

Let's not leave our Judaism at the door when we leave the synagogue and just pick it back up the next time we come back. Rather, let's take it home and keep it with us at all times by making it an integral part of who we are. We must engage ourselves by taking advantage of all that Judaism has to offer, ritually, socially, educationally, spiritually, morally, the list goes on. By doing so we have not only answered the question of How To Be Jewish, but we've answered the question Why Be Jewish as well. We have shown Judaism to be a force for good, of fostering caring people and caring communities, and we have shown that there is not only one right and true way to be Jewish. Rather, there are many, many ways to be Jewish and to preserve our Jewish identities.

THE BUSH STILL BURNS   8

The Torah describes the familiar image of the burning bush with the words, "V'hasneh einenu ookal," "And the bush was not consumed!" In God's first revelation to Moses He made it clear that, just as the bush was not consumed by the fire, so too, the Jewish people will not be consumed, for God is always with us. As we know all too well, for thousands of years, the Pharaohs of every generation, their names may have changed, but their goals have remained the same, have tried to destroy us. However, these words, and the symbolism of the burning bush, represent God's promise to us that just as the fire didn't and couldn't destroy the bush, so too, the Egyptians and their descendants will not be able to destroy the Jewish nation.

That is how the symbolism of the burning bush is usually expressed. However, that symbolism lulls us into a false sense of security. We look at the burning bush and say, okay, we've lasted for all these years despite hardship and persecution. Thus, we are optimistic that we will continue to survive. After all, isn't that what God had promised us?

In taking this attitude, in understanding the symbolism of the burning bush in this light, we fail to recognize one important aspect. We fail to see that we, each of us, individually and collectively, must do our part to see to it that the bush does not die out; that it is not extinguished. To put it another way, each of us must have a piece of that bush burning inside us. Each of us must do our part, take a branch or a thorn even, and do whatever we can to keep it aflame, because if we don't, then we can't expect God to do His part.

This is the example we learn from Moses. On three separate occasions Moses turned God down when God asked him to assume the mantle of leadership of the Jewish people. Moses' response? He wasn't prepared. He wasn't worthy. He was slow of speech. It sounds just like the excuses we hear all the time from people who don't want to get involved; who don't want to assume positions of leadership, or who don't want to even join a synagogue. Don't pick me they say. Pick somebody else. Let somebody else do the job. By having this attitude, we run the risk that nobody else will do the job, and so the job doesn't get done. Imagine, if you will, if Moses had walked away from that burning bush. We probably would still be slaves in Egypt!

Yet God didn't give up on Moses and Moses didn't walk away either. Moses came to realize that he was chosen for a reason. That reason has everything to do with the symbolism of the burning bush. Perhaps Moses was chosen at precisely that location, with that bush burning in the background because it represented an aspect of Moses which we often overlook but one which we must all have. Despite his statements and protests to the contrary, Moses had that fire burning within him, as evidenced by his killing of the Egyptian task-master, to do what he could to help the Jewish people.

This is what we still need today. We need people, who, while perhaps not rising to the level of Moses, still have the burning desire to do good for the Jewish people and not to let that flame, that fire, be extinguished. Fortunately there are such people, probably thousands throughout the world, certainly not modern day Moseses, but average, ordinary people, who keep that bush still burning. It takes many, many people to keep the bush from being burned out and it takes many, many people to do their part to keep the Jewish people alive.

Unfortunately, we live in a world where, while it might be easier to be Jewish, it is increasingly more convenient not to be Jewish; not only because of the problems of inter-marriage and assimilation, but because we encounter far too many people who see no need for the bush to keep burning; who see no need for a distinct Jewish identity. Unfortunately, it seems as though there are more people out there who want the bush to burn out than there are potential Moseses who are doing their part to preserve the Jewish community. This is why, those of us who care, must do our part, each one of us, even in small ways, to maintain our Jewish identities, and to keep that fire burning within us, so that the bush is never extinguished.

Sometimes we feel that we can't do this singlehandedly. Sometimes we feel that it's not worth the effort. However, as we learn in Pirkei Avot, "Lo alecha hamelacha ligmor;" while it is not up to us to complete the task, we are not free to shy away from it either. We must all do our part, because every little piece helps; because it's the unsung people who really strengthen the Jewish community, who do their part to make sure that that bush continues to burn and is not extinguished.

We learn from Moses' experiences that people are human and will let us down at times. Yes, even Jewish people, and yes, even leaders and stalwarts of the Jewish community. However, like Moses, despite our frustrations working or volunteering within the Jewish community, we can never give up. We can never stop.

What is the symbolism of the burning bush? It's the idea that no matter what hardships we encounter, the flame will never be extinguished; the bush will never burn out; and the Jewish people will never die. But only, only, if we each carry that flame, and a piece of that bush inside us.

PART II

GROWING CLOSER
TO GOD

GOD'S VOICE

1

Although we are familiar with the stories at the beginning of the Book of Genesis; the stories of creation, Adam and Eve, the Garden of Eden, and Cain and Abel, knowing these stories is not enough. We must also understand why these stories appear and what lessons we should take from them. Furthermore, we should train ourselves to read and study these stories with an adult perspective rather than through a child's eyes.

We know that Adam and Eve made a big mistake in the Garden of Eden by eating from the fruit of the Tree of Knowledge of Good and Evil and that Cain made a big mistake by killing his brother Abel. We also know how Adam and Eve were punished for their sin by being expelled from the Garden of Eden, and Cain was punished for killing his brother by becoming a marked man. As children, we might learn from these episodes that if you don't listen to your teacher you can get expelled from school, or if you are not nice to your brother you can get kicked out of the house. As adults, however, we should pause and ask more serious and deeper questions.

If God told Adam if you eat the fruit you will die, why didn't God kill Adam immediately? If Cain killed Abel, why wasn't he killed? Where's the punishment for these sins?

In order to answer these questions, we need to take a closer look at the true nature of the sins or crimes which were committed. In Adam's case was his sin eating the fruit? Was Cain's sin killing his brother? This is what we were taught as children. Perhaps, though, they both did something else wrong; something which, while maybe not as egregious, is certainly something we all do in our lives, something which we can, and should, avoid doing.

What happened after Adam and Eve ate the fruit of the Tree of Knowledge of Good and Evil? They hid from God. So God called to Adam and said, "Where are you?"

Adam answered, "I heard Your voice in the Garden, and I was afraid because I was naked, so I hid."

God asked, "Who told you that you are naked? Did you eat from the tree which I commanded you not to eat?"

Adam replied, "The woman that you gave to be with me - she gave me to eat from the tree."

So God said to Eve, "What is this that you have done?"

Eve said, "The serpent deceived me, and I ate."

It's the blame game! It's almost comical if you think about it. If this was a play, we'd think it was slapstick comedy, with each character pointing behind them, placing the blame on the next one. However, this incident was not so funny. We know the consequences it ultimately brought.

Similarly, after Cain killed Abel, God spoke to Cain and asked, "Where is your brother." Cain's famous reply; "Am I my brother's keeper?"

As evidenced by God's conversations with Adam and Cain, these two incidents have something important in common. As Rashi explains, God obviously knows what Adam has done. He obviously knows what Cain has done. Yet God does not immediately attack either Adam or Cain with an accusation. Rather, God strikes up a seemingly innocent conversation with them, asking in a gentle, non-threatening way, "Hey Adam where are you?" "Cain, how's your brother doing?"

One would think that the vengeful, punishing God we read and hear about, would be more than happy to come right out and accuse Adam and Cain of some impropriety. One would think this vengeful God would even punish first and ask questions later. But God didn't do that.

Instead He spoke softly. He had a conversation with them. By doing so, God gave both Adam and Cain a chance to admit their mistake, and to express regret. Did Adam get the hint? Did Adam stop and think for a moment and come clean to God? No! Did Cain? Not him either. Instead Adam hid from God and Cain denied responsibility.

God knows we're not perfect; He created us this way. God knows we will all make mistakes, and that we will all sin at some point in our lives. This is why he created mechanisms for atonement and forgiveness. However, God expects us to take responsibility for our actions and admit when we've done wrong; because without doing so, there is no hope to correct it in the future.

We tend to think of the voice of God as a threatening one, yelling at us, judging us, and hitting us over the head with a hammer. That is the voice of God we associate with the High Holidays. However, we learn from Adam and Cain's encounters with God, that even if we sin, in the beginning, God speaks to us in a whisper. He speaks to us in conversational tones. He talks to us kindly and patiently.

This is the voice of God we want to hear; the softer voice. This voice which tells us we don't have to hide from Him; a voice which tells us that He understands if we sin, but He will still be there and will forgive us, especially if we are willing to admit our wrongdoings and not hide from Him. On the other hand, if we do hide from Him, if He has to go and find us, He might not be so forgiving. God's voice will be much louder, much more imposing, much more vengeful. But yet, He still wants us to admit our guilt, and yes He will still forgive us.

With which voice do we wish God to speak to us; the voice of Adam, or the voice we associate with Rosh Hashanah? If we want God to speak to us the way He spoke to Adam and Cain, if we want to have that kind of relationship and conversation with Him, then the lesson from the Garden of Eden is not, "don't eat the poison apple," but rather, if we do, and odds are we will; don't run away, but admit our guilt, and continue to engage in a conversation with God.

In addition, it is up to us to hear that voice all year round. We do so by staying with God throughout the year, praying to Him often, and following His commandments. The more we communicate with Him, the more we engage with God and our faith, the more we will hear that softer voice of God. And the more we hear that voice, the more we will want to continue the conversation.

VOICES OF TORAH   2

There are numerous ways of reading and understanding the Torah; many interpretations by which we let God, through the Torah, speak to us. I believe the best way to read the Torah, especially portions which we question, don't understand, or feel are meaningless or irrelevant, is with an eye and an ear firmly planted in the present time. It means letting the Torah speak to us in a voice we can understand and appreciate, and which makes sense to our own eyes and ears as we read and hear it.

I believe the idea of listening to God in a more modern way first came from Moses, who realized, at the end of his life, as he went about explaining the Torah to the new generation of Israelites, that he had to do so in a way that his audience would understand. For example, we can look at the Ten Commandments. No, not the original version; but the one forty years later, where Moses described to the people the events which took place at Mount Sinai, and then repeated the words which were spoken by God at that time.

Moses did this because he was addressing the next generation of Israelites, the one which would now be entering the
Promised Land. The generation which received the original Ten
Commandments, which had left Egypt and was at Mount Sinai
to experience God's words, had all died. But in so doing, Moses
changed the words of the Ten Commandments; the words God
had spoken forty years earlier. At Mount Sinai God said, in the
fourth commandment, "Zachor," remember the Sabbath day,
the Shabbat. But in Moses' version, he said "Shamor," observe,
the Sabbath day. What is the significance of this change?

While the Lecha Dodi prayer provides us with an explanation - "Shamor v'zachor b'dibur echad" - both words were
uttered by God at the same time - if we examine the words
more closely, we see there is a subtle difference between the
two, different meanings because a different generation was
listening to the message.

In the original version, the one we read in Exodus and on
Shavuot, we are commanded to remember, "Zachor," Shabbat,
because God created the universe in six days and rested from
His activity on the seventh day. Because God rested, so we
too must rest. By resting, by ceasing from creative activity,
we acknowledge God's role in creation.

But in Moses' version, we are commanded to observe,
"Shamor," Shabbat, for an entirely different reason. We
observe Shabbat to remind us of our past; to remind us of our
slavery in Egypt. We observe Shabbat to remember that when
we were slaves we had no days off. Therefore we must ensure
not only ourselves, but our servants as well, a day of rest.

Zachor or Shamor? Does it matter which is the correct
reason for remembering/observing Shabbat? Perhaps not.

But understanding why Moses made this change helps us to understanding how God still speaks to us today, and how He wants us to understand His message in every generation.

The generation which experienced slavery and the subsequent Exodus needed no reminder of those events. They only needed to remember - to "zachor" - that God created the world. However, the generation which had not known slavery, is told to observe - "Shamor." This generation, which is now about to enter the Promised Land and face the challenges of founding a nation, is in a very different place than the generation of their parents who had witnessed the events at Sinai. The lessons learned from the experiences of the Exodus will be different for those who actually lived through those events than for their children and their grandchildren. Moses realized this and changed the words of the Ten Commandments to suit his audience.

This raises some questions, however. What right did Moses have to change the word of God? Did he do so deliberately and with God's permission? The answer is yes. Moses indeed had God's permission. God also realized that He needed a different message to this new generation. He needed to impress upon them the importance of the slavery experience because they hadn't experience it. God thereby tells us that while His message is timeless, the manner of communicating it and understanding it changes with each passing generation.

This is why the Torah stresses that the covenant between God and the Jewish people is eternal. This covenant was not only made with the generation who had left Egypt. It exists for the next generation and for all subsequent generations as well. Its provisions were transferred to their offspring to be realized by them in the new land. It is a covenant that was made with every single one of us. Those who were standing at Sinai and those who are living today.

How do we get subsequent generations to understand and fulfill their part of the covenant? How can we get today's generation to do the same as well? The answer is by following Moses' lead. Moses, speaking for God, related his version of the Ten Commandments in a way that would be more meaningful and understandable to his audience. In this way, he hoped they would "observe," "shamor," the commandments, because he knew they couldn't remember. They weren't there.

God has given us a book - the Torah. That Torah relays our history, our experiences, and the way to relate to God. It's all in there, for everyone and for all time. But in order to keep that Torah, in order to keep it fresh and relevant, we have to be willing and able to change its voice as is necessary for each new generation.

The generation which left Egypt heard the Torah in one voice. The generation which was about to enter the Promised Land heard it in another. Every generation since has studied and applied the same Torah, but with a different voice appropriate for that particular time and place.

We have all experienced Judaism a particular way in our lives. Our parents might have experienced it a different way. Our children and grandchildren might be experiencing it another way. This is all perfectly acceptable. The Judaism of our parents does not have to be the exact same Judaism of our children. The Judaism of our childhood does not have to be the same Judaism of our adult years. What matters is that it's still Judaism. What matters is that we still practice and study it, still engage in both "Shamor" and "Zachor," still hear God speak to us, thousands of years later.

WHERE IS GOD? 3

When we reach the latter part of the Book of Exodus, following the plagues, the crossing of the Red Sea, the Ten Commandments, etc., we might feel as though we are watching the Oscars. We have categories for Best Actor - Moses, of course; Best Supporting Actor - Aaron; Best Director - God; Best Costume Design for the High Priests' clothing; and Best Set Design for the building of the Tabernacle in the desert.

Much of the latter half of the Book of Exodus is concerned with the details involved in building the mishkan, the tabernacle, where the Israelites worshipped while wandering through the desert. Although the details of the construction of the mishkan are of little practical concern to us today, the concept of the mishkan, which later became the Holy Temples in Jerusalem, and which, following their destruction, evolved into the present synagogue, is still very important and relevant.

Why is that? Because, to use a movie reference again, "If you build it, He will come." We don't really believe that if we were to build a tabernacle, or a Temple, or a synagogue, then God will miraculously appear, like out of a field of corn, make Himself visible to us, and then permanently reside there. We know movies are fiction; not reality. Therefore that vision, that image, is not to be. This is one major difference between the movies and our approach to God.

As much as we value the Temple and the synagogue, they are not the end all and be all of our religion. And as much as we feel God's presence in the synagogue, that is not enough either, because God is not only in the synagogue. We believe that God is to be found everywhere.

To quote an old Hebrew School song,

"Hashem is here, Hashem is there, Hashem is truly everywhere.

Up, up down, down, right left and all around,

Here there and everywhere, that's where he can be found."

We believe that God is everywhere, not just in one particular place, no matter how holy that place is. To reinforce this concept, the commandment to build the mishkan is worded in the Torah as follows, "And they shall make Me a sanctuary so that I shall dwell among them."

The Torah does not say "So that I shall dwell in it." Rather, it says, "So that I shall dwell among them." What's the difference? The sages explain that through the mishkan and now the synagogue, God rests and dwells within each and every Jew, within each and every one of us.

If this is true, if God is always with us wherever we go, why do we even need a synagogue to pray to Him? Why do we even need organized religion for that matter? Is God any more inside a synagogue than He is on the street? Do we not believe in an infinite God who is everywhere? Why is there a distinction between the synagogue and elsewhere?

The answer is that although there shouldn't be any difference, we nevertheless make that distinction ourselves. If we define God as only being in one particular place, the synagogue for example, we also define, and create a place where God isn't.

Judaism, however, does not want us to think or act that way. Yes, it's important to have a synagogue, a Temple, or a tabernacle, but only because we need to feel that God is here somewhere on Earth. At the same time, we should remember even an invisible God is indeed everywhere.

The Temple, and the synagogue, are not glorified palaces for God, and they are not a home away from home for God. God doesn't need us to build Him a place to reside in this world. He already resides everywhere. God doesn't need the Temple or synagogue. We do.

The synagogue is not a place where we store Him away, only to take Him out when we need Him. It would be very convenient to put God in the Temple and worship Him, speak to Him, and have a relationship with Him there, because that is where He is. But in the rest of our lives? There is no room for God. This is why we say that God doesn't dwell in it, but among us. God isn't only in our lives when we come to worship Him. God is always in our lives.

The truth is, sometimes we do need to come to a particular place, the synagogue, to feel His presence. Hopefully we do feel His presence when we come, and hopefully that presence will be enough to sustain us when we leave. It is why the role of the synagogue is to inspire us to a develop a closer relationship with God.

This can be accomplished in many ways. A word of wisdom here; a beautiful melody there; a line from the liturgy that strikes us. Or it can just be sharing the experience with friends, and receiving comfort from them when you need it most. While that inspiration lifts us for the moment, we must figure out a way for that inspiration to remain with us, after we have left the building and returned to our day-to-day lives. This is because, as the saying goes, if a synagogue does not inspire us, there is a problem with the synagogue. But if the inspiration lasts only as long as we are in the building, then there is a problem with us.

The feelings of warmth, friendship, togetherness and Godliness which we experience in the synagogue, or wherever we come together to worship God, must remain with us after we leave the building and after the services are over. It remains with us only if we realize that God too remains with us and that He is always with us. God is truly everywhere. But most of all, He dwells within each and every one of us.

Altars And Synagogues

4

Immediately following the recitation of the Ten Commandments God tells Moses that the people should not worship Him by making gods of gold and silver but by making an altar of earth, a plain altar on which to perform the sacrifices. God doesn't want the fancy altar, the fancy stone, and the fancy synagogue. God wants us to worship Him with simplicity. The sacrifices are important; the prayers are important; a person's real feelings are important. Not the setting, and not the trappings.

This commandment teaches us that worship should be spontaneous and personal. Sometimes we experience or feel a strong desire to communicate with God, to thank Him, or to request His help with a personal problem or situation. When we have these feelings, we should not hesitate to express them. We shouldn't be bound by time or place or status.

The Torah contains numerous examples of this type of worship, including the stories of Cain and Abel, Noah, and the patriarchs, all of whom thanked God for fulfilling His promises to them, by erecting altars, or offering sacrifices as the mood struck them. Abraham was the first person to recognize and pray to the one true God. He didn't need a synagogue, a fixed liturgy, or clergy. He just prayed to God when he felt it was appropriate. He would build a simple altar whenever he wished to offer a sacrifice in whatever place he found himself. God certainly approved of this method of worship because, as was stated by the Prophet Nehemiah, in words we recite in our liturgy every morning, God found Abraham's heart true before Him, "U'matzata et levavo neeman lifanecha." Abraham, the perfect man of faith, is certainly the ideal man of worship.

Knowing this, doesn't it seem a bit odd that God nevertheless instructed Moses to build a mishkan, a tabernacle, a place where God can dwell among the people? If that wasn't enough, God even gave Moses detailed instructions on how it is to be built, and, what's more, with what materials it was to be built! Not just regular stones; not just plain earth. The tabernacle, the place to worship God, was made of gold, silver and copper. It was made from the finest wood, yarn and linen. The altar itself was made from acacia wood with copper horns. Nothing but the best for God's dwelling.

Why did God go from the original ideal of simplicity, from the ideal of individual spontaneous worship, to the seeming ostentatious? What can we learn from why that switch took place? The following incident helped me understand.

A friend of mine once remarked how he hates the fixed routinized prayers of the synagogue. Like Abraham, he would prefer the spontaneity of worshipping God, of being alone with God, to commune with God in solitude, to pray to God when he was at the beach or on a mountain, admiring God's role in nature.

Sometime after that conversation, I was invited by friends to their summer house in North Carolina. One Sunday afternoon we went to the top of a particular mountain where we could see the many mountains of the area. Recalling the conversation about communing with God precisely at moments like these, I looked out at the mountains, admiring the scenery, and began to daven Mincha.

It didn't work. I didn't feel any closer to God. I actually didn't feel anything. Why not? Because I needed a shul, a chapel, a minyan, ten Jews mumbling to each other. That to me is the essence of worshiping God. Being with others. Community. Fellowship. This helps to explain the change which took place from the Abraham model of private worship to the communal model of the Sanctuary.

In the desert we became B'nei Yisrael. We became a community; a nation. Our worship of God couldn't only take place in our own backyards because we are not all like Abraham. So we have a tabernacle. We will later have a Holy Temple and the synagogue. We will have a sacrificial system. We will have priests to officiate. It is all part of our evolution; part of learning to be a community, learning to pray with each other and for each other, and learning not to be selfish and only pray for ourselves.

We can easily understand this evolution and why it was for our benefit. However, there was one aspect in the building of the Tabernacle which seemed to take this idea a bit too far - the types of "gifts" which were required for the construction of the Tabernacle. Only the best and top of the line; only the most expensive were brought.

Doesn't this send the wrong message, that our synagogues must be made of the finest and most expensive materials? Doesn't this make synagogues more expensive and cost prohibitive, and in the process drive many Jews away? Doesn't this separate the haves from the have nots?

While the answers to all these questions might be yes, there is a reason why God only wanted the finest and best materials for His sanctuary, a reason which applies all the more so with our synagogues today. Just as we take pride in our own homes, just as we want the best for ourselves and our own lives, we should take that same pride in, and want to beautify the synagogue, the same way.

To do so for ourselves, for our own homes, doesn't take much out of us. After all, it's for our own benefit. To do so for a synagogue, however, to do so for something which is not solely our own, for something so many others, even strangers, will benefit from, is a sign of caring about others. It is a sign of trying to benefit others, making others more comfortable, making the community stronger.

We have a word for that. It's called "chidur mitzvah," the beautification of the mitzvah. It teaches that it's not enough to just donate for the upkeep of the synagogue, but we must try to go that extra mile, to beautify the synagogue, to make it a place we can be proud of, just like our own homes. In so doing we also remember those who sacrificed of themselves to make the synagogue possible; who donated the fine materials; who donated not just money, but time and effort. By looking around the synagogue we should be inspired by those who made it happen and it should inspire us to continue their work, and to make it our own, by continuing to give as well. Yes, it takes money, and yes it takes sacrifice.

Without realizing it, many people today behave like Abraham. They pray to God whenever and wherever they please. They don't realize that God has given us, commanded us, a different way of worship. One that brings us together, teaches us the values of community, sacrifice, respect, beautification, Holiness, and ultimately the sanctification of God's name, through our actions and generosity.

This is why God commanded us to build a place of communal worship. Not so that we can show off, not for our own egos, not to be ostentatious, and not to separate the haves from the have nots. Rather, to bring us together, to inspire and elevate us, and to bring us even closer to God. It's a system that even Abraham would agree will make a person's heart true and faithful to God.

PRAYER 5

Despite what we recite in our prayers, and despite how often we might pray, for many of us, it is still difficult to relate to God. No matter how often or how hard we pray, we really have little understanding of God and how He relates to us and the world. This is why it is sometimes difficult to feel His presence or understand His role in our lives. Furthermore, since God has no needs, since He doesn't need our prayers or our praises, and since we can't bribe Him with anything, why do we pray?

The answer is we pray for one reason alone. Not to change God, but to change ourselves. We pray so that we may gain the courage or the strength to change. We pray to teach us the humility which comes from having to plead for something. We pray so that if our request is granted, it might lead us to maintain that attitude and pass it along to others.

Does this mean God isn't listening, that our prayers are in vain, or that they are unanswered? No. Our prayers are always answered by God. They just aren't always answered in the way we expect, not always as quickly as we hope, but one of the most crucial aspects of prayer is learning to accept the fact that when we pray, sometimes the answer is, "No."

God might say "No" to us for a number of reasons. If granting our request would hurt either ourselves or others, God will not grant that request. When God decides that something we have prayed for shouldn't be granted, or shouldn't happen, then we pray for something else. We pray for the wisdom to understand why. An important part of our spiritual growth is learning to accept "No" as an answer and learning to accept graciously what we cannot or should not change.

By accepting that sometimes the answer is "No" we also learn that prayer is not a substitute for human effort. When we were in school and had a big test the next day, didn't we pray to God to get an A? Didn't we promise to be good little boys and girls if we got an A? Of course we did! We also did something other than praying to God. We studied for the test. We didn't just rely on God to answer our prayers.

When we asked God to give us that A, what we were really asking Him for was the strength to study, and the ability to understand and remember the material. This is quite different than merely asking something from God without putting in any effort of our own. If we prayed to God for an A, and we got a B, or heaven forbid a C, that didn't mean that God didn't answer our prayers, or that He didn't listen. It meant that God heard us, but that His answer was 'No." Moreover, He gave us that answer with a message. That message is, next time study harder!

Sometimes, however, God does answer our prayers even when we don't ask for His help. A number of years ago, Murray, my synagogue's gabbai, had gone to a store to purchase a sink to use for washing our hands. For various reasons the sink didn't fit, so he went back to the store to return it.

Unbeknownst to Murray, the store had a no refund policy. At most they would give him store credit and he could purchase something else. He explained that he purchased this sink for a synagogue and might they reconsider their policy. The man at the return desk told Murray the store policy, but also informed him that aside from working at this store he was also...... a Minister. Because the sink was purchased for a religious use, the minister suggested that Murray pray that the store refunds his money. Murray told the minister that he doesn't pray for these types of matters.

Lo and behold, the store agreed to take back the sink and refund the money! The minister came over to Murray and said, "You see, it's a good thing you prayed; it obviously worked." Murray replied that he hadn't prayed. "That's okay," said the minister, "I prayed that you would get the refund."

As they say, God works in mysterious ways. As I say, we never know when and to whom God is listening. Prayer is important. It is our best, if not only, way of communicating with God. So long as we pray we know that God is always listening, and that if we pray often enough, if we communicate often enough, the answer to our prayers is YES.

SIXTH SENSE 6

E ach year over the summer, my synagogue holds an ice cream social. We do that because, as we've come to learn, people really like ice cream. Grown men and women actually colored in pictures of ice cream cones with crayons. One reason for our excitement over ice cream is that ice cream appeals to each of our senses. We like looking at it, we like smelling it, we like touching it, and of course we like tasting it.

But do we really use all of our God given senses? Do we use each of them to make us fuller people, and in particular fuller Jews, or do we only limit ourselves to maybe one sense; the one we're most comfortable with, or satisfied with? Thinking of those who don't have use of all their senses, either because of a physical or mental impairment, should be motivation for us to make the most out of the senses we are blessed to have, to not only maintain them, but to try to heighten our other ones as well. Because each of our senses has some relation to Judaism, we must strive to use all our senses to become more complete and fuller Jews.

Some of us are taste Jews. We like our Jewish foods. We like our bagels. Yes, we even like coming to shul for ice cream. We can do more though. We can't be satisfied with having our bagel on Sunday morning and therefore think that we have done our Jewish thing for the week. Instead, we could have ourselves a taste of Judaism. We can have a traditional Shabbat dinner and try to eat more kosher foods and support the kosher establishments in the area. You'd be amazed at the diversity of kosher products on the market.

Next is the sense of hearing. Some of us are Shema Jews. "Shema Yisrael Adonai Eloheinu Adonai Echad." We know that line well and so we might listen to God and think we are obeying Him. Today we have stopped listening to Him, and we have stopped listening to and conversing with each other. Instead we listen to our Ipods. So let us go back to Shema. Let us become better listeners and listen more closely to those around us. We need to listen more closely to the voice of God which speaks to us every day, if only we let Him in. At the same time, we need to listen more to His commandments and of what God wants from us.

The next sense is sight. We need to open our eyes more and see the good and beauty in Judaism. We cannot focus solely on the negative and the difficult. We need to open our eyes to new ideas and new possibilities to enhance our Jewish lives and future. Someone came up with the idea of Birthright, sending young adults on free trips to Israel. That was due to the sense of sight - foresight; of looking for ways to make not only our own lives but our Jewish lives better and brighter.

Then there is the sense of smell. Yes we can smell the aroma of different foods, like a challah baking in the oven; we can smell the spice box from Havdallah. However, we must heighten our sense of smell, to be alert and aware of what's going on in the world around us. We cannot be complacent, and rely on others to protect us and save us. If we smell danger, we must respond accordingly and not wait until it's too late.

The final sense is touch. Yes, we touch and feel those tangible items of our Judaism, like the Torah. However a heightened sense of touch means wanting to, and being willing to, touch others, because it's how we touch others that ultimately comes to define who we are. We must reach out and touch our fellow human beings.

These are just some ways of heightening our senses so that we can live more fuller lives as Jews. But there is yet another sense out there. Our Sixth Sense.

This sixth sense is not ESP or some paranormal or psychic ability. Our sixth sense is how we envision God and His role in our lives, and how we relate to God. While God is not reachable through our physical senses, he is nevertheless reachable through that sixth sense which we all have. We must begin to develop our sixth sense in order to develop a better relationship with God.

We begin by understanding that our relationship with God cannot be based solely on fear. We cannot be afraid to reach out to Him or to get too close to Him because we might fail; and if we fail God, then surely we have much to fear. Rather, we need to see God not as some all-powerful entity who is sitting waiting to judge and punish us, but as someone to get closer to and to reach out to.

Our relationship with God must exist to bring us a sense of comfort and strength. It is why we are also commanded in the

Shema to love God. Our relationship with God must also be based on love. We should always strive to get closer to God, to climb that proverbial stairway to heaven. This should be our continued goal and purpose in life; to always reach and aim higher.

Sometimes, in our efforts to reach higher, we slip and we fall. That is okay because doing God's will is not an all or nothing proposition. Judaism is a process, a journey, where every step counts. That is what God asks of us. To engage, rather than disengage, in that process; to go on that journey, instead of staying home.

Fully developing a sixth sense about God, developing a more personal relationship with Him, means we should always strive to do more for Him and at the same time not to feel guilty or discouraged if we don't. Do not let people accuse you of being a bad Jew because you don't do things perfectly, or their way, or 100% of the way, 100% of the time. As long as you are making the sincere effort to reach higher and reach God, you will succeed.

Instead of looking at God as someone to be in constant fear of, look at God as a friend or mentor. Look at God as someone who inspires us and gives us choices in life; as someone who truly cares about us. Look at God as a personal GPS system, which guides us on the path we should follow, but is always willing to help us if we go astray.

If we can change our attitude towards God, if we can become closer to God through love and not fear, we can also use that same approach in our relationships with the people we encounter in our lives. For if we do, our entire lives, not just our Jewish lives, will be that much more fulfilling. It is therefore our choice if we only wish to rely on just one sense, or if we'd rather use and develop all our senses in order to become fuller Jews, better people, closer to God, and in the process, better enable us to meet life's challenges.

A HANUKKAH MESSAGE 7

The Talmud tells us that the one true mitzvah on Hanukkah is "Pirsumei Nisa," publicizing the miracle. It's not enough that we merely light the Hanukkiah; we place it on our windows so that others can see, in order to publicize the fact that we are Jews. One way to do so is by following the example and behavior of Joseph, who believe it or not, was the first to teach us how to observe Hanukkah.

When Joseph's brothers were sent to Egypt by their father Jacob to obtain food, Joseph accused them of being spies. Despite their protestations that they were "honorable" men, Joseph nevertheless had them imprisoned for three days. Joseph freed them on condition that they go back to Canaan and bring back their youngest brother, Benjamin. Jacob had originally refused to send him, because he couldn't bear losing him as he had thought he had lost Joseph. To ensure that they would do so, Joseph kept Simeon as a hostage.

Why would the brothers believe that Joseph would uphold his end of the bargain? Anticipating this thought, Joseph said,

"Do this and you shall live, for I am a God fearing man." Joseph used those words for two reasons. First, to let us all know that he still maintained his Jewish identity. He hadn't lost it despite being away from his father's house for over thirteen years. Second, Joseph hinted to his brothers who he was. He was trying to get a reaction from them; if not by recognizing that he was their brother Joseph, at least by recognizing that they shared a common God.

So he said, "Did you hear me? I fear GOD! I believe in GOD!" Joseph told his brothers that he feared GOD. Not the sun god, not any Egyptian god, not Pharaoh, but GOD. Elohim! The Hebrew GOD!

We might think that after hearing this the brothers would have questioned this claim. They might not only have asked Joseph how he knew of Elohim, but also responded that they too were God fearing, that they too were Hebrews. But they didn't. They were too caught up in their mission, even their guilt over what they did to Joseph, according to the Midrash, to notice. Their fear of God, their acknowledgement of God, their identity as Hebrews, never came up.

It is ironic therefore that Joseph, the Vizier of Egypt, still spoke of his God, but ten Jews, a minyan if you will, failed to acknowledge theirs. Subsequently, when the brothers returned to Egypt and questioned why they had extra money in their bags, the steward, who the Midrash identifies as Joseph's son Manasseh, stated, "Do not be afraid, your God, the God of your fathers, must have put treasure in your bags for you." The brothers' responded to this acknowledgement of God with Silence! Later, when Joseph met Benjamin, and said, "May God be gracious to you," what was Benjamin's response? Again, Silence. At no time did the brothers publically acknowledge their God, despite numerous invitations to do so.

In our retelling of the Joseph story, these conversations are usually omitted. However this dialogue and this debate between those who claim that they are God fearing and who acknowledge God on the one hand, and between those who don't acknowledge God because they have seemingly more important things on their minds, is a metaphor for the Hanukkah story. Hanukkah is the battle between those who want to retain their Judaism and those who want to assimilate and be guided by the secular world; the battle between those who fear God and those who fear something else.

This is why Joseph's proclamation that he is a God fearing man teaches us how to observe Hanukkah today. Joseph was fulfilling the Hanukkah mitzvah of publicizing the miracle, when he said I am a God fearing man. He was symbolically placing his Hanukkiah in the window so that his brothers would see. He was telling his brothers that it's acceptable to acknowledge one's Judaism in public, even if one is in the minority. Joseph said to his brothers, what we say to some in our community today, "Are you more fearful of God or are you more fearful of the possible backlash or repercussions by being too visible as a Jew?"

While they were afraid to publically acknowledge they were Jews, while they would much rather have blended into Egyptian life and gone back home with their grain, Joseph wouldn't let them. Pharaoh, his advisors, Joseph's underlings, all knew that Joseph was Jewish. Yet, despite the cultural and religious differences, they nevertheless respected him for it. Perhaps the Hanukkah miracle was that Joseph somehow managed to rise from lowly slave and prisoner to a position of supreme power, all while retaining his Jewish identity and faith and not assimilating.

We saw the consequences of the brothers' silence when confronted with their heritage, when they returned to Egypt with Benjamin and were invited to dine with Joseph. They were not permitted to sit at the same table with Joseph because Egyptians weren't permitted to eat with Hebrews. This should signal to us that we can hide our Judaism all we want, and we can light our menorahs only in the privacy of our own homes so nobody else will know, but we are still Jews. That can never be hidden or forgotten.

Since this is our reality, and since we can't escape from it, we must therefore be willing to publically acknowledge that we are Jews. We must be willing to publically light our menorahs and we must be proud to be Jewish. We shouldn't be fearful of God, but trusting of God so that we have no qualms in standing in Pharaoh's palace and acknowledging that we are Jews. After all, isn't that what Moses did years later? He proudly stood in Pharaoh's court, as a Jew, and said let my people go to worship God as we see fit.

This is exactly what Joseph had in mind when he said, "I am a God fearing man." This is what Moses said years later. This is what the Maccabees said many centuries later under their circumstances. This is what the Jewish people have been saying ever since, through hardship, persecution, exile, and near annihilation. We are God fearing people. We believe in God. Elohim. And we are not afraid to say that or to show that.

Hanukkah can be understood in this light. Not just in the light of dreidels and latkes and gelt, but in the light of acknowledging that we are a God believing people, and acknowledging that we have the freedom to worship that God.

What is the point of having that freedom if we don't use it? Joseph used it even though it wasn't Hanukkah. Moses argued for it even though it wasn't Hanukkah. And the Maccabees fought for it so that we can always celebrate Hanukkah.

Hanukkah serves as a reminder of God's miracles in every generation and of the victory of religious freedom over religious persecution. It serves as a reminder of the spirituality and peacefulness of candles burning in the window and of how Judaism can be practiced and observed in the home. Hanukkah serves as a reminder of the victory of the few over the many, an allusion to the modern State of Israel.

The dialogue which Joseph began with his brothers has continued throughout the ages. We cannot be silent like Joseph's brothers. Rather, we keep the dialogue going by speaking the words of Joseph, telling everyone that we too are God fearing people.

This is the message of Joseph, of Moses, of Judah Maccabee, and of all who came after. It is now our message and our obligation; to remain God fearing men and women, and never let the light go out.

TEBOWING 8

Joseph, the eleventh and favorite son of the patriarch Jacob, has more of his life story written about in the Torah than do Abraham, Isaac and Jacob combined. Yet while Abraham, Isaac and Jacob are considered patriarchs, Joseph is not. Nevertheless, in rabbinic lore, he is considered a Tzaddik, a righteous person; Yosef HaTzaddik. However, it's hard to imagine Joseph, especially the young Joseph, as a tzaddik. He would go out in the field to see what his brothers were doing, and then run back to tattle on them to his father. He was not the least bit modest about being his father's favorite son and walked around wearing an amazing technicolor dreamcoat. He was not the least bit reticent about having dreams or delusions of grandeur, seeing himself as a sheaf with the other sheaves, symbolizing his brothers, bowing down to him, or as the brightest star with the sun, the moon and eleven other stars bowing down to him. If that wasn't enough, he had the chutzpah to boast about these dreams to anyone who would listen. If all this wouldn't make you want to hate Joseph, throw him in a pit, and sell him to traveling Ishmaelites, then nothing would.

Despite these beginnings, Joseph's later behavior showed us why he is called a tzaddik. After being thrown into the pit and sold into slavery by his brothers, Joseph was bought by Potiphar, one of Pharaoh's chief advisors. Soon enough, because of his talents and abilities, Joseph became the head of Potiphars's household. But Joseph never took the credit for his newfound status. He always gave the credit to God. It was God's will that he was separated from his family and put in that position. When Joseph was thrown in jail based on Mrs. Potiphar's false accusations, Joseph rose to become the head prisoner. He interpreted the dreams of the baker and the cupbearer. Because of his skill and ability in managing a household and a prison, Joseph was admired and respected by all those he came in contact with.

Through it all, the good and the bad, the admiration for Joseph and his righteousness didn't come about because he accumulated any wealth or material possessions for himself, or because he gave out gifts to members of the staff. Rather, it came about for two reasons. First, he had faith that God would guide his endeavors and lead him to success. Second, because of the way he treated others. Joseph was no longer the tattle tale or the one with delusions of grandeur. Joseph behaved in a way that led others to want to be around him, to respect him, and to listen to him. Joseph inspired others to do and be their best. After all, isn't that what a righteous person should be about; inspiring others through their actions and beliefs?

Joseph was a tzaddik because he kept telling everyone, Potiphar, the baker, the cupbearer, even Pharaoh himself, that his gifts and talents were not his, but came from God. We too should give credit to God for our successes, as well as being inspired by those who also succeed and give credit to God, rather than take that credit for themselves.

Here's a modern example. If, like me, you happen to have a child who attended the University of Florida, you have been subjected to all kinds of messages about the Gator football program. This was because they were led by a quarterback of supposedly superhuman, God-like status, by the name of Tim Tebow. What made Tebow so noteworthy was not only his success on the football field, leading his team to two national championships, but his strongly held evangelical Christian beliefs, which he was never hesitant to discuss or display.

Tebow graduated, and was chosen in the first round of the draft by the Denver Broncos football team. He was laughed at because he didn't throw the football the way an NFL quarterback should throw it. He threw it, as one reporter wrote, "like a frisbee." He was doubted because he didn't have the physique of a traditional NFL quarterback. They said he was drafted as some sort of publicity stunt.

But in the 2011 season, with his team doing poorly, Tebow became the starting quarterback. The Broncos were 1-4 at the time. Led by Tebow, the Broncos won seven of their last nine games and made the playoffs. Most of those wins came on exciting last minute drives or in overtime.

As Mike Lupica of the Daily News wrote, "Now I just sit back along with everybody else and wait for the last two minutes of these games and watch him take his team down the field and win again and end up cheering my head off along with everybody else." And that seems to be what was captivating the nation. How this man, of seemingly modest talent, was suddenly able to carry his team to victory after victory!

Asked after every game how he did it, Tebow simply thanked God; and his teammates, of course. Sound familiar? Didn't Joseph do that thousands of years ago?

Tebow believes in God. He is a religious person and he is not afraid to let everyone and anyone know that. For this he has drawn much criticism. He is criticized for praying before, during and after games. Images of the way he poses, genuflects, bows, now known by the term "Tebowing," are shown and mocked all over the world. Tebow has become a lightning rod for all those who find public displays of faith and religion somehow threatening or even offensive.

What we really should be focusing on, however, is not Tebow's beliefs, but his actions. Leading by example, not browbeating others to pray or believe as he believes, and defying all the odds to succeed, should inspire us.

Given all the bad stories we read about in the newspapers, in sports especially, it is not only refreshing, but inspirational and optimistic to read about a Tebow for a change. Wouldn't we rather read, watch, and follow a person who does well, achieves beyond his abilities, thanks God for that success, and makes others around him better, than read, watch and follow another sports figure being arrested for violent crime, drugs, or sexual abuse of minors? Yet Tebow is criticized for being a good role model; all because he displays his religious beliefs publically.

Put aside the specifics of Tebow's religious beliefs and it all boils down to the same thing. Like Joseph, Tebow inspires others. To some, it's through his beliefs; but to most, especially his teammates, it's by his actions, his belief in them, his optimism, and by his inner conviction and faith that when the pressure is on, he will succeed. As former football coach Jimmy Johnson said, "Tebow is the best I've ever seen at bringing out the best in the people around him."

Tim Tebow may have questionable skills but he doesn't doubt himself. Like Joseph, he has the strength to do what he knows is his job to do. He believes that God will see him through. There is nothing wrong with that. This is why, as people of faith ourselves, no matter how Tebow's career ultimately pans out, we should draw inspiration from what we have witnessed on the football field, and use that as inspiration to live our lives with the Jewish values our religion dictates.

Joseph is called a tzaddik because he inspired others; through his faith, through his actions, through his talents, through his modesty, through his ability to elevate others, and most of all by recognizing and acknowledging that all his success came about because of God. It is why we learn from him and try to emulate him

At the same time, while it may be sacrilegious for Jews to be "Tebowing," we can still learn from him as well. We can learn about how he professes his faith and how he leads his life, both personally and professionally. And we should use that knowledge as inspiration to engage ourselves, as Jews, in a little more "Josephing;" that is being righteous, being a tzaddik, and bringing more light, faith and Godliness into this world.

KNOWING GOD 9

The words "Shema Yisrael Adonai Eloheinu Adonai Echad," the classic statement of Jewish belief, six words which are taught to every Jewish child, and which every Jew knows by heart, sum up our belief in the existence of one God. But despite these words, as Jews, it's not as important what we believe, as what we do. Specifically, we are to follow God's commandments. We are to do mitzvot, not just sit around saying we believe in God.

If someone asked you to explain what Jews believe, what would you say? How would you answer? Would you say that Jews believe that Saturday is the day of rest? Or would you answer that eating pork is prohibited? Either one of those answers is not a statement of belief. They are statements describing what Jews do or don't do. These examples reinforce Judaism as a religion of action, not a religion of belief.

This brings me back to the Shema. It is probably the most important statement of Jewish belief - the belief in one God. Yet even the great rabbinic commentators couldn't agree on what it means. Some commentators even claim that this verse does not preclude the existence of other Gods. It just infers that we only worship one God whose name is Adonai. And our usual translation of this verse, "The Lord is Our God, the Lord is One," only came about in the Middle Ages in response to Christian claims that the Shema alludes to the Catholic idea of the trinity.

Belief is a very difficult concept. It can mean different things to different people. However, aside from the differences between action and belief, there is another difference which might help us explain how Judaism looks at the idea of belief. This is the distinction between belief on the one hand, and knowledge on the other. There is a difference between what we know and what we believe.

For example, we believe in many things. Belief is faith. Belief is hope. Remember Tug McGraw of the 1973 New York Mets and his famous slogan, "Ya Gotta Believe?" He was expressing his faith, his desire, and his hope, that the Mets would win the pennant.

But while Tug might very well have truly believed in his heart that the Mets would win the pennant, did he really know that they would? Of course not.

This is why knowledge is different than belief. To know something is to be certain of it. We know, don't we, that 1 + 1 = 2. That's not a matter of belief or faith. It's a fact. Tug McGraw might have believed, and we might have believed with him, but he didn't know for certain, he couldn't have known for certain, as an absolute matter of fact, that the Mets would win the pennant that year.

By way of another sports example, contrast Tug McGraw with Joe Namath guaranteeing a victory in the Super Bowl or Mark Messier guaranteeing a victory in the Stanley Cup playoffs. Did they believe or did they know? Of course they couldn't know for sure that their teams would win. However, based on their respective experiences and abilities, their guarantees were not statements of belief but, to them at least, and for their teammates and fans, they were statements of knowledge.

And it is this knowledge which is at the heart of Judaism. As Maimonides says, as Jews, we don't just believe that there is one God. We know that there is one God. And it is this knowledge of God, rather than the belief in God, which the Torah continually reinforces.

Take the Ten Commandments. How does it begin? "I am the Lord your God who brought you out of Egypt." For the generation of Jews who were brought out of Egypt, and who received the Torah, they "knew" that God, Adonai, did in fact lead them from slavery.

They didn't just believe it. They knew it. They felt it in their minds and in their hearts. They witnessed God firsthand in the plagues that fell on Egypt, at the Red Sea, and finally at Mount Sinai.

And there's more. The Torah contains many references to the idea that we should come not just to believe in God, but to know God. For example, we read, "Know therefore that the Lord your God, he is God, the faithful God, which keeps covenant and mercy with those who love him and keep his commandments to a thousand generations."

The Torah doesn't tell us to just believe, just merely have faith that there is God. It wants us to truly know, not only that there is a God, but to know God as well.

We express this concept, this knowledge of God, in our prayers; specifically the "Aleinu" prayer which we recite at the conclusion of every service. In English we read, "It has been clearly demonstrated to you that the Lord alone is God, there is none beside Him." In Hebrew it reads, "Ki Adonai Hu Ha'elohim, Ein Od Milvado."

More to the point, also from the Aleinu prayer, we sing, "V'yadata hayom, v'hashevota el levavecha." It is translated as "Know therefore this day, and consider it in your heart, that the Lord is God in heaven above, and upon the earth beneath; there is no other."

The Torah, especially the book of Deuteronomy, is filled with references to knowing that there is a God, knowing God, and knowing what God has done for us and is capable of doing for us. And we have gained this knowledge not through belief, and not because of belief, but through and because of our experiences. And it's that knowledge of God, not just belief in God, that we strive to attain whenever we recite the Shema, study Torah, or observe Mitzvot.

So how do we get to know God rather than just believe in God? The answer is that knowledge is borne by experience. It's a knowledge which is born from living a Jewish life. The more we experience this world, the more we experience Judaism in all its facets, the more we come to know God.

And that is what we strive for as Jews. Knowledge of God, not merely believing in God.

This is why, stating that there is only one God is not just a statement of belief. It is a statement of knowledge. It's a statement of fact. Hopefully we come to not only believe in God, but to know God, and to share that knowledge with others. And hopefully we have come to know that belief is shaky, belief is temporary. But knowledge is firm and everlasting. Especially when it comes to God.

And it's not just our experiences of thousands of years ago, which give us this knowledge, but it is also our experiences today, witnessing the rebirth of the State of Israel, for example, which shows us that God fulfills His promises.

So let us not just come to believe in God, but let us strive to know God. Like the generation which left Egypt and experienced God first-hand, let us truly come to know God in our hearts and in our minds and let our life experiences, studying Torah, doing mitzvot, and seeing God's hand in all that we do, further sustain us in that knowledge.

PART III

HERITAGE AND TRADITION

FAITH AND CHESED 1

We read and hear a lot about that concept we call "faith." But what exactly is "faith?" Abraham is considered to be the perfect man of faith. This claim is made for many reasons, not the least of which was his willingness to sacrifice his beloved son Isaac because God had told him to do so. However, looking at Abraham's life, we see what faith really is about, and that perfect faith involves more than merely believing in and trusting God. This is why Abraham is not only considered to be the model of faith, he is also considered to be the model of chesed, of kindness.

Who was Abraham, and why has he had such a lasting impact on us thousands of years later? Abraham was chosen because he was the first to believe in the idea of one true God. Seemingly out of nowhere, God told Abraham "Lech Lecha," leave the country of your birth, of your ancestors, and to go to a new land where you will become the father of a great nation. Abraham, the man of faith, naturally did so without hesitation.

But once Abraham arrived in the Land of Canaan and settled there, we see how he was deeply concerned with the comfort and well-being of others. His tent was always open to any and every wanderer. He gave his nephew Lot the first choice of land to settle. He left his sickbed when he saw strangers in the distance, ignoring his own pain in order to show them hospitality. He pleaded with God to spare the people of Sodom and Gomorrah.

Through these actions, Abraham's faith in God as well as his kindness and chesed also had an effect on others, specifically members of his household, who also learned and acted with these values. For example, when Abraham sent his servant Eliezer to find a wife for his son Isaac, Eliezer didn't ask God to find a woman who was beautiful or wealthy, he asked God to find Isaac a wife who exhibited the trait of chesed, of kindness and compassion. Eliezer asked for a girl who was not only ready and willing to offer him a drink of water, but to offer water for his camels as well. He found such a girl in Rebecca, another model of chesed.

When we examine Abraham's life, we see that Abraham did not live by faith alone. He lived and served God by and through his actions. For Abraham it was faith in God combined with chesed towards man which made him the father of a great religion. This is why God chose Abraham, the man of kindness, rather than the man of faith, to pass on to his children the dual paths of both faith and morality, and it is why Abraham is the father of the Jewish people. We, as Jews, are entrusted to emulate Abraham's actions, his chesed, and not just his faith in God.

While faith might indeed sustain us, faith is nevertheless individual. It is selfish. It only helps ourselves. Faith alone does nothing to help others. But like Abraham, chesed, kindness, is how we use our faith to help others, to be ethical and moral, and to do our part in tikkun olam.

This model of both faith and chesed is not only practiced by Jews. A number of years ago, thirty-four Chilean workers were trapped in a coal mine for sixty nine days. When rescued, they spoke of how their faith in God sustained them throughout their ordeal. But these miners did not survive on faith alone. They survived because they were kind, considerate, and compassionate to each other, and because of the kindness of others. They survived because of the tireless efforts and ingenuity of those who tried to save them, and because of the food and medicine that was supplied. Faith can only take us so far. The rest depends on chesed, on our own kindness, and on the kindness of others.

When the elevator was finally ready to take the miners out, an argument ensued. One would think that the miners argued about who would leave first because they couldn't wait to get out of that mine, but that would be wrong. The miners argued because they didn't want to be the first to leave. They each had faith they could survive a few more hours, and they also had the chesed, the compassion, the kindness, to understand that perhaps it was more important for one of their fellow miners, perhaps one in greater need of assistance, to leave first. This trait of kindness, of true chesed, was so powerful that it even trumped the human need for freedom. If we are truly people of faith, then witnessing these acts of kindness should continue to solidify our faith; not only in God, but in the goodness and kindness of our fellow man as well.

This incident can teach us an important lesson. The next time we have to wait at a red light, or for an elevator, or in line at a restaurant, or at a checkout line, or at the bank, think of the Chilean miners and how they acted when they had to wait, certainly under more trying circumstances. Then look for someone who is having trouble waiting and let them go first.

They say that a pessimist is one who sees the glass as half empty and an optimist is one who sees the glass as half full. That may be true, but Abraham would see that glass and ask, "Is there anyone here who is thirsty? If so, let me bring him some water." This was the way of Abraham. This is the way of chesed. This is the moral, ethical and just way. It is how true people of faith should act.

Stairway To Heaven 2

We're all familiar with Jacob's dream of a ladder, a stairway to heaven, complete with angels, traveling up and down that ladder. It is a vivid image which we can all imagine in our minds. It's an image and a dream which has been the subject of much commentary, not only because of its significance, but because it lends itself to much insight into how to better our lives, and how to better our relationship with God.

Jacob's ladder is significant to our Jewish lives because the rungs on the ladder represent our different levels of observance and commitment to Judaism and to God. Just like the angels who go up and then go down that ladder, so too do we try to elevate ourselves. Sometimes we go up, and unfortunately, sometimes we go down. But we should at least be on that ladder, making the effort to be more observant and more committed to our religion and to God. Better to be on the lowest rung of the ladder than not to be on it at all!

Unfortunately today, too many of us aren't on the ladder, much less on the lowest rung. This is because we see no use for it. We don't have the time or patience to get to God via a ladder because we live in a world where things move in a hurry; where everyone wants a quick fix; where dial-up internet, unheard of even twenty-five years ago, is no longer good enough because it's not fast enough. We live in a world where we want instant gratification, and we want it in the easiest way possible. We don't want to work for it. We just want to snap our fingers and, poof, like magic, it's there! Because so much of society is accessible like that, we expect it, and we demand it, in every aspect of our lives, including religion and our relationship with God.

Think of those who have a fascination with Kabbalah. It's "spiritual," they say. It's connecting with God through Jewish mysticism, and connecting with God is what it's about! We don't have the time, patience or inclination for ritual or learning. It's all about finding God.

Those who espouse this view believe they have a unique and amazing ability to take the express elevator straight to God; straight to heaven. They believe that they have God's e-mail address and cell phone number, and can even text message Him. That is what our society tells us. We don't need ladders Ladders are old-fashioned. Ladders are yesterday. Ladders are slow and tedious. We have new technology, new ways of reaching God. And once we get there, we can easily stay there.

Jacob's ladder, in fact, Jacob's entire experience, teaches us otherwise. First, bear in mind that if the angels - God's messengers - can't stay at the top of the ladder; if they can't stay in heaven with God, but have to return to earth; have to come down, we shouldn't think that we are any better, that we can just go right to the top and stay right at the top.

Jacob's ladder teaches us that getting to heaven, getting closer to God, involves many steps and rungs. It teaches us that a ladder is not an elevator even if both can eventually get us where we want to go. Through the trials and tribulations of his life, Jacob comes to learn that reaching the top of the ladder does not come easy; neither for patriarchs, nor for angels. It's a process. One rung at a time.

It doesn't happen unless we make a concerted effort to make it happen. It takes time, patience and understanding. Today, we no longer have that patience. The funny thing is, neither did Jacob. If we want to restore some patience to our lives, look at what Jacob's dream was really all about. Go beyond the image of the ladder for a moment and actually focus on the dream and its aftermath.

At the conclusion of Jacob's dream, God blesses him and promises that his offspring will be numerous and will inherit the land of Israel. This so called dream is in reality a prophecy. It's actually God communicating with Jacob just as he communicated with Abraham and Isaac. God offers Jacob the exact same promise and blessing that he offered them.

When Jacob woke up, when he was ready to resume his journey, he made a deal with God. He said if God will protect me, if God will provide me with food, clothing and shelter, if God will bring me back home safely, then, God will be my God. As an added bonus, I will give God 10% of my earnings (after taxes of course). After receiving an unconditional blessing and promise from God, Jacob responded with a conditional promise in return!

Why did Jacob make these conditional promises in return for God's unconditional one? Why did he pray for material things? The reason was because God's blessings and promises to Jacob were long term promises. They were in the future. They had no real meaning to what Jacob was going through. They might have convinced him in the end it would all work out, but at the time, Jacob needed more. He wasn't worried about his future. He was worried about his present. Jacob didn't have the patience to see that life is a process, and there are steps which must be taken to get to where you want to go.

And so Jacob said to himself, "Yes I know God promised me a bright future. Yes I know God promised that a great nation will be descended from me. That's all well and good, but how is that going to help me solve my immediate problem? How is that going to help me reach Laban? How is that going to protect me from Esau? Children? Future generations? God, how about I find a wife first??"

In our own age of instant gratification we too are not likely to make a real effort, not likely to invest our time and effort, or even believe in something, if we know the results won't be seen for quite some time. To put it another way, the incentive of immediate reward is more enticing than the long term benefit.

We all have short attention spans and we sometimes lack the patience we need to realize our long term goals. We lack the patience we need to climb up the ladder; step by step and rung by rung. We only seem to have time for the elevator. Jacob was no different. Since God didn't promise him anything concrete, in the here and now, something Jacob wanted and needed at the moment, Jacob felt he needed to make a deal with God. Hence the conditional promises. Hence the "if!' "If" God does X, then, and only then, will I do Y.

Although Jacob did not have patience when he first encountered God, as evidenced by his reaction to his dream, over the ensuing years, as Jacob had to deal with Laban's deceitfulness, and he had to work more years than he anticipated, he learned patience. He learned what it truly means to await God's promises and blessings. He learned why that ladder was important and he learned how to climb that ladder. This is why when Jacob reached the end of his life many years later, he was able to look back and realize that God's blessings and promises had in fact come to fruition, even if they didn't come as easily or as quickly as he would have liked.

We learn from Jacob that even in our fast paced, instant gratification, I want it now world, we must slow down, exhibit patience, and realize the many blessings we have in our lives. We do so by taking the time to climb the ladder and not always being in such a rush to take the elevator. Just like you can't build or paint a house without a ladder, so too you can't reach God without that very same ladder. It's the necessary tool to reach God. So keep that ladder with you and remember it is truly the stairway to heaven. But only if you use it!

ANGELS 3

After twenty years away from home, Jacob left his Uncle Laban and returned to the Land of Canaan, but not before he was met by an angel who wished him well on his way. The appearance of an angel was ironic, because when Jacob first set out on his journey he also had a dream about angels; the afore-mentioned dream of angels climbing up and down a ladder. The appearance of angels as bookends to the Jacob story is a good time to ask about the role of angels in Judaism and in our lives.

In the television program "Touched by an Angel," Della Reese played the chief angel who was assisted by two young apprentice angels. They came to Earth in human form to intercede in the lives of people who needed help with something in their lives. At the end of each episode, when they successfully helped the person in need, they revealed themselves as angels, and were suddenly surrounded by special effects, bathing them in bright light.

This fictional depiction of angels is how we normally think of them; as having an aura, a halo, or bathed in bright light. However, this depiction of angels is not only unrealistic, it's not very Jewish either. Only in Hollywood do angels appear with special effects. Yet angels are not Hollywood actors, and they are not solely as depicted in many pieces of art, shining like the sun.

Our texts and liturgy make constant references to angels. In the Kedusha, in the Amidah, we recite, "Kadosh, Kadosh, Kadosh," a re-creation of how the angels praise God. The idea of the Kedushah, which means holiness, is that by reciting the lines the angels recite, we are striving to be like angels, praising God. During the Shacharit service our prayers make reference to various forms of angels. We recite "V'haophanim V'chayot Hakodesh B'ra'ash Gadol, Mitnasim L'umat Serafim, L'umatam Mishabchim V'omrim." That one line alone makes reference to ophanim, to chayot ha-kodesh, and to seraphim, all of which are categories of angels in Jewish lore.

The most famous example of angels in our liturgy is the "Shalom Aleichem" prayer, which is sung on Friday nights. According to the Talmud, two angels accompany us on our way back home from the Synagogue on Friday night – one good angel and one evil angel. If our house has been prepared for Shabbat, if the candles are lit and the table set with wine and challah, the good angel blesses us that the next Shabbat will be the same, and the evil angel responds, "Amen." If we come home from the Synagogue and our house has not been prepared for Shabbat, the evil angel wishes that the next Shabbat will be the same and the good angel responds "Amen."

Think of the words to that prayer;

"Shalom Aleichem, malachei hasharet, malachei elyon;

Boachem l'shalom, malachei hashalom...;
Barchuni l'shalom...;
Tzeitchem l'shalom....

Each of these stanzas refer to the idea of angels; angels of God, messengers of God, and angels of peace. Perhaps this is why, according to the Zohar, Jewish mysticism tells us there resides in each of us a good angel and an evil angel. Our every step is therefore guided and accompanied by both good and bad angels. Jewish mysticism also teaches that even in the next world angels accompany man where, depending upon our life on earth, we are received either by the angels of peace or by the angels of destruction.

On a more practical and less theological level, Judaism offers us two ways to see angels today. The first way involves elevating ourselves in holiness, to become more angelic and hence more Godlike. The second way involves seeing angels in others, who exist in our lives to help us through difficult times, who enlighten us, and who brighten our lives.

Returning to Jacob's dream of angels climbing up and down a ladder, it is significant that the Torah states, "Olim v'yordim bo," the angels were first climbing up the ladder and only then coming down, because it signifies that the angels were first coming up from earth to get to heaven. This is the way in which we too typically climb ladders. If the angels are truly going up to heaven from earth, this might just mean that their origin is in the earth below rather than in the heavens above. This idea suggests that angels, divine messengers, are of possible earthly origin and therefore truly in our midst. To put it another way, angels are human; and angels are truly among us. Our neighbor could be an angel. Or perhaps a family member. Or a friend.

Too often we have preconceived notions, believing for instance that Godly acts are sent from one direction only - from heaven down to us on earth. Instead, perhaps we should think of the possibility that the word of God or Godly acts originate here on earth and not in heaven. That goodness and godliness just might originate from each one of us. This is why we must always act like earthly angels of God, inspiring others to holiness, bringing others closer to God, and helping others with the ups and downs of life.

Using this definition, we must also open our eyes to the possibility that God does send us angels, even today. Today they appear in human form, in the form of those who we encounter in our lives. Sometimes these angels serve to bring us closer to God. Sometimes these angels appear at just the right time, when we need them the most. Sometimes these angels are just there for comfort and support, to help us out of difficult situations, to provide encouragement and joy, to brighten our days, and to offer unconditional love. Other times they inspire us in so many ways, to be and to do our best, because when we allow others to brighten our lives, then we know that there are truly angels among us.

We never know when these angels come into our lives, but when they do come in, hold on to them, for they are special people and don't ever let them go. If we do see angels in others, if we do truly appreciate how they have helped us, then we should take some of that inspiration, some of that angel dust, and use it to be angels for others. This is how we can make earth a little more like heaven; by being angels and climbing that ladder.

AND DEMONS 4

If the previous chapter was about angels, this chapter is about the opposite... Demons.

As much as we like and want to believe that we have angels in our lives, the fact is that we are also plagued by demons. No, not the devilish creature kind, but those things that really bother, annoy and aggravate us, and thus harm us greatly, as we go on with our lives. And Jacob was no different.

When Jacob left Canaan to live with his Uncle Laban in Paddan Aram, he left alone. He had no one with him. But when Jacob returned home after twenty years, he returned with two wives, two handmaidens, twelve children, and an abundance of livestock and riches. Life was good, just as God had promised.

However, Jacob was the ultimate skeptic. Jacob couldn't accept all the good in his life. He always had to look behind him, paranoid; afraid, for example, that his brother Esau was still angry, and still wanted to kill him. It was this fear of Esau which led Jacob to divide his camp into two parts, thereby ensuring that Esau couldn't defeat his entire family.

One night, we are told, "Jacob was left alone." Jacob had a large family, and plenty of servants and possessions; but Jacob was left alone. Theologically speaking, the words "Jacob was left alone" come to mean that Jacob suffered from his own particular demons, and although he tried to let God and others as well, into his life, he had a hard time appreciating them and keeping them there. Jacob forgot what had happened to him twenty years earlier. He forgot his dream of the ladder and he forgot his own reaction to that dream, which was "Surely the Lord is in this place, and I was not aware of it." In Jacob's mind, God was not with him. By his own doing, his family wasn't with him either. Jacob was therefore alone.

This was Jacob's problem and it is also a problem for many people today. We too have moments when yes, we recognize God in our lives, but too often, we don't. We don't thank Him for the good. We agonize and blame Him for the bad. We also have moments when we recognize those people in our lives who love us and care for us. Then, as with God, when things go bad, we shut them out. We say they can't help; we say that we are alone; we feel abandoned. We don't even ask, "God where are you?"

God had done everything Jacob had asked of Him. He kept up his end of the bargain. Jacob had food, clothing, and protection, and was a few miles from home. Yet Jacob still felt alone, for the same reasons we too feel alone even when in truth we are not. Like us, Jacob still had not fully grasped God' role in his life. He still hadn't fully grasped, despite everything that had happened to him, "Surely the Lord is in this place, and I was not aware of it."

While all this was going on in Jacob's mind, while Jacob was "alone," he met a man. Or was it an angel? They wrestled and fought until morning. While this struggle is ripe for comment and interpretation, whether it was Jacob's inner struggle or a real fight, why it occurred, etc., perhaps it was a real encounter; a message from God. Maybe it was a slap in the face; a wake-up call; tough love. Maybe it was God's way of finally getting to Jacob. The symbolism of ladders didn't work. Realizing that God was in this place didn't work for Jacob. Maybe he needed something else.

What did Jacob need? Jacob needed a physical reminder of God, not an amorphous, spiritual one. And he got it alright! The angel wrenched his hip socket; his sciatic nerve. Jacob was left with a permanent limp from then on; a permanent reminder of God. If Jacob didn't know "Surely the Lord is in this place, and I was not aware of it" before, if Jacob didn't know that God was still with him, that he was not alone, then he certainly knew it now. He would never forget that God was with him. He had a permanent scar to prove it.

So it is with us. We all have within us an inner Jacob, our own demons, our own fears and feelings of being alone. We are all filled with doubts about God and even about people. What we learn from Jacob is that it's okay to have these doubts. As long as we remember that, while we may never fully erase the Jacob within us, it is within our power to overcome him.

Today, we can't expect God to appear to us, or to engage in a wrestling match with us. This doesn't mean God is not in our lives. It doesn't mean God isn't in this place. It doesn't mean that we are alone. What it does mean is that we have to work harder to find God. God has given us the tools to find Him; to say "Surely the Lord is in this place, and I was not aware of it."

One of these tools, perhaps the foremost tool, is prayer. We pray to communicate with God. If we do so, especially in the synagogue, or communal setting, we will find that others are there too; that we are not the only one praying; that we are not the only ones saying Kaddish, for example. In other words, we are not alone. This is why, even if we can't find God through prayer, hopefully we can find some friendship and compassion and camaraderie.

As a Jew we are never alone. God is always with us. We've got brothers and sisters around. We're part of a family, whether we choose to believe it or not. So believe it and cast those demons away. Or to paraphrase a song from the Broadway show Jekyll and Hyde, "May this be the moment, when we send all our doubts and demons on their way." If we cling to God and to His people, then we will truly "never walk alone."

No Jew Left Behind 5

We're all familiar with the famous line from the Torah, "Let My People Go." It's a line which has been repeated throughout history as a rallying cry for freedom; whether it be for the Civil Rights movement of the 1960s or the Soviet Jewry movement of the 70s. It's a line which speaks of physical freedom. The Torah however does not merely say "Let My people go." Rather it says, "Let My people go.... so that they may worship Me."

According to the original screenplay, Moses asked permission from Pharaoh for the Israelites to go out into the desert, take some animals, and sacrifice them to their God. Moses even tells Pharaoh that they'll only be gone for three days. Pharaoh considers it, but ultimately refuses the request. Then right before the eighth plague, the plague of locusts, Pharaoh's advisors are ready to give in. They advise Pharaoh to let the Israelite men go to worship God. So Pharaoh considers this request and confirms with Moses who's going; assuming that only the men are going.

In a phrase from the Torah, perhaps more important than "Let My People Go," Moses replies to Pharaoh, "B'naareinu u'v'z'keineinu nelech, b'vaneinu u'biv'noteinu, b'tzoneinu u'biv'kareinu nelech, ki chag l'adonai lanu." Moses tells Pharaoh, not just the men are going; but everyone is going. We will all go, says Moses; the young and the old, our sons and daughters, our flocks and our herds. Moses says, in essence, if we can't all go, none of us are going. Pharaoh then dismisses Moses and we know that God again hardens Pharaoh's heart and more plagues follow.

This phrase, "With our young and with our old we will go, with our sons and with our daughters we will go," "b'naareinu u'v'z'keineinu nelech" - is actually a very important Jewish concept and ideal because it sums up exactly what it means to be a Jew. Moses insisted that everyone be included in the miracle of the Exodus. He wasn't satisfied that only the men leave or only the elders leave. He would only be satisfied if everyone left. If the children left, if the older people left, and yes, even if the animals left.

The phrase "B'naareinu u'v'z'keineinu nelech" speaks volumes about the character of the Jewish people, both then and now as evidenced by the movie "Defiance," the true story of a group of partisans hiding out and fighting the Nazis during World War II. The heroes of the film were two brothers, the Bielski brothers, whose parents were murdered by local Nazi sympathizers. They originally ran into the forest in order to escape and save their own lives. But in the process of escaping and fighting, they encountered many others, fellow Jews of all ages, sexes, backgrounds, skills and abilities. Young, old, male, female, healthy, sick, skilled, unskilled, observant, unobservant - it didn't matter. They were all taken in and res-cued by the Bielskis, who oftentimes risked their own lives to do so. According to the film, approximately twelve hundred Jews were saved.

Why were these Jews saved? Because the Bielski broth-ers realized what Moses realized. If we are to leave, then we all must leave. No matter how difficult the journey would be, no matter the disputes and fights along the way, no matter that provisions would be scarce, winters cold, and illness and death would certainly follow, they are our fellow Jews, and no one will be left behind.

Moses understood, as must we today, that we are all part of one larger community. We must fight for and support the goals of the community, and do so without having to resort to petty divisiveness. Divisiveness was Pharaoh. It was how the Egyptians did things. It was not how we, the new Israelite nation, did things, nor is it how we Jews should do things today. We are all-inclusive. Everyone has a stake, everyone has a role to play, and we will not leave anyone who wants to be a part of it behind.

"B'naareinu u'v'z'keineinu nelech." By uttering those words, Moses showed the Egyptians what a true leader was. He was the type of caring leader they craved. The type who would not allow them to be ravaged by plague after plague. He could have left with only a few men, but he didn't. He stayed until every man, woman and child would leave with him.

This is why when the people did leave, "Chamushim alu bnai yisrael memitzayim;" they left with the eruv rav. It is claimed that almost one-fifth of those who left Egypt were not Israelites. Rather, they were Egyptians and other foreigners who were drawn to Moses because he cared for all the people, not just himself, and not just the important people.

Moses' actions teach us that there is room under this big tent we call Judaism for everyone. There is room and a place for the young and the old, the new and the existing. There is room for a variety of practices and traditions, and opinions and beliefs, and all should be respected.

Unfortunately today, too many people and denominations, both religiously and politically, believe that their way is the only way; and that inclusiveness is meant only for those who believe and act as they do. They should step back and take a lesson from Moses. He made sure everyone had a place. He wouldn't leave Egypt unless everyone and everything could come along.

"B'naareinu u'v'z'keineinu nelech". A few simple words. It doesn't make for great dramatic dialogue, but it goes a long way in teaching us to care about others and include them in what we do. It reminds us that "Kol Yisrael arevim zeh lazeh," that all Jews are truly responsible for one another.

It doesn't matter whether you're a Moses leading a million people out of slavery, or a Bielski brother, a modern-day Moses, leading twelve hundred people out of the hands of the Nazis. Whatever we do, we do it together as Jews. Every Jewish life is important, and no Jew will be left behind. That is the Jewish way.

SPEAK LOUDLY AND CARRY A SOFT STICK   6

Following the death of Moses' sister Miriam, the well which had provided water for the Israelites in the desert dried up. The people complained to Moses that they had no water. Moses in turn called out to God who instructed him to speak to a rock and have it bring forth water. However, instead of speaking to the rock, Moses struck it. God punished Moses for his disobedience by not allowing him to enter into the Land of Israel. Moses' sin? He failed to exhibit the necessary faith in God in front of the entire nation.

While we can question whether the punishment meted out by God fit the crime, a better question to ask is why did God tell Moses to speak to the rock in the first place. Furthermore, why didn't Moses follow God's instructions, as the Torah tells us he did every other time he was told to do something? In order to answer these questions, we need to put them in the proper historical context.

Approximately forty years earlier, after leaving Egypt, the Israelites first complained about their lack of food and water. At that time, God told Moses to "Smite the rock and draw forth water." Moses of course did as he was told. He hit the rock with his staff and water gushed out. Thus, forty years later, when faced with the same problem, it would be natural to think that God would give the same instruction to Moses, and that Moses would want to repeat his success from earlier.

With this in mind, we might rephrase the first question to read, not why did God instruct Moses to speak to the rock, but rather, why did God change the instruction from striking the rock to speaking to it? In this light, the second question now becomes why did Moses exhibit the same behavior as forty years earlier? Why didn't he change in accordance with God's instructions?

The answer to the first question, why did God change His instructions, lies in the differences between the two events forty years apart. The events we've read or know about have involved Moses taking action. Moses struck and killed the Egyptian taskmaster; he used his rod to bring plagues upon Egypt; he lifted his arms to part the Red Sea; he smashed the Ten Commandments. Forty years earlier, he hit the rock to have it bring forth water.

These physical actions were what the people who had left Egypt, that first generation, had come to expect. They were physically beaten by the Egyptians. They had a leader in Moses who was used to lifting his hands and taking action. So they understood and responded to Moses' actions in hitting the rock.

A generation or two ago, it was the accepted practice of the rabbi or teacher to hit a student on the knuckles with a ruler if he was misbehaving or uninterested because that's how youngsters responded. Can you even begin to imagine the outcry if a teacher were to hit a student, even lightly, in order to get his or her attention today? Times have changed; attitudes have changed; the way we react to certain stimuli has also changed. We therefore must realize that there is a time for force and a time for speech. The first to understand this and adapt accordingly was... God! The person who did not adapt and change was... Moses.

God understood that this new generation, those who did not grow up under Egyptian slavery, would not respond to the "hitting" approach. This generation, which had grown up in freedom, required the softer approach of "speaking." This is why God told Moses to use his staff in order to speak to his stiff-necked people. To speak to them and not strike them. To persuade them and not to overpower them. God saw that sometimes there is a need for diplomacy and sometimes a need for force.

Then was the time for force. Forty years later was the time for diplomacy. It was the time for a softer approach. It didn't make one approach better than the other. It merely meant we needed to keep our options open and take the best approach that the times demand.

Moses didn't speak to the rock because he couldn't adapt. Moses was not a talker. He was slow of speech. He was reluctant to go to Pharaoh. He was reluctant to become the redeemer of the Israelites because that would involve talking. Despite what God told him to do, Moses still hit the rock. Not once. But twice! First, Moses hit the rock and no water came out. It was God's message to him that hitting won't work this time. At that moment Moses had the chance to reconsider and to perhaps think about what God had actually told him. He didn't. He couldn't. So he hit the rock again.

Moses couldn't change his ways or adapt to the new circumstances. Like so many of us, he was set in his ways. He had hit the rock forty years earlier. In his mind that was how we did things. We've always done it that way. Why should it ever change?

This is precisely the attitude of so many today. Why should I change? Why should I adapt? It worked this way before. It will work this way again. It's an attitude that pervades so much of our lives, especially religion. I've always prayed this way. In my shul up north we always did it this way. It's never been done before, etc.

As we see, the lesson is that it doesn't always work the same way. God stepped forward to teach us this lesson which Moses and many of us still fail to grasp. We fail to listen to the voice telling us to try another way, to try something different. In the words of the Life cereal commercial - try it, you'll like it.

This was God's message. "Listen Moses, there might indeed be a different way of doing things. Don't be so closed minded and stubborn. Try something new. It just might work. It might not be better, but if it gets the desired result.....".

As a leader, Moses failed to realize that the current generation needed something different. They needed to be spoken to rather than be hit. Because Moses failed to adapt, because he was still stuck on what had worked forty years earlier, he sinned. He disobeyed God. He demonstrated a lack of faith in God in front of the entire congregation. In the process he demonstrated why he was not the person who should lead the people into the next stage of their journey; to conquer the Promised Land.

Moses and the people ultimately did learn this lesson. They asked permission of Sichon, king of the Amorites to pass through his land, offering to pay for any damage. In other words, they spoke. They engaged in diplomacy. When they were turned down, when they realized that diplomacy wouldn't work, only then did they take action and fought.

Ultimately, the episode of the rock comes to teach us to be cognizant of our circumstances, be flexible in our approach to many of life's challenges, and be open to new ideas and concepts.

Bringing The Mashiach 7

The Shabbat before Passover is known as Shabbat Hagadol. It gets its name from a line in that morning's Haftorah, where the Prophet Malachi says, "Lo, I will send the prophet Elijah to you before the coming of the great and awesome day of the Lord." This "Yom Gadol," great day, is understood to signal the beginning of the Messianic age. As we know, because it appears so often in our liturgy, God will send the prophet Elijah to usher in the Messianic age. Thus, Shabbat Hagadol, represents our hopes and prayers that God will indeed send Elijah, and will indeed send the Mashiach.

What is this Messianic age about? What will happen when the Mashiach comes? In the final verse of this Haftorah, God reveals Elijah's role in the redemptive process: "And he will return the hearts of the fathers to the children, and the heart of the children to the fathers." In other words, in this ideal messianic age, parents and children will be reunited, and families will live in peace and harmony. The rabbis elaborate on this concept by telling us in the Mishnah that Elijah's arrival will finally bring justice, peace and harmony not just to individuals, not just to families, but to all nations and to all the world. This is why we pray for the arrival of Elijah and for the Mashiach.

This is wonderful, but what has to happen for the Mashiach to get here? How do we usher in the Messianic age? How do we go about convincing God to send Elijah in the first place?

The answers to these questions lie in the Passover holiday. On Seder nights, we can't merely be satisfied that we've invited Elijah to our homes, he came through our doors, and had a sip of wine, before we sent him on his merry way to the next house.

The Seder is an appetizer; it's a tease. God sends Elijah, just as He promised, but to truly usher in the Messianic Era, we must get Elijah to stay, by giving him a reason to stay! How?

One way is by paying attention to the details of the holiday, and doing the work necessary for its fulfillment. We can't ask God to just send Elijah and let us live in a world filled with peace and harmony. To bring in the Messianic Era we can't take the easy way out and we can't just sit back and do nothing. We can't say, "don't make me work on my relationship with God, don't make me put any effort into my religion, don't make me engage in anything remotely connected to Tikkun Olam."

Instead, Elijah comes to our homes to see if we even made a Seder, if we in fact paid attention to details, and if we engaged in the work necessary to really and truly usher in the Messianic Era. When Elijah comes to our homes, he wants to see what we've done. Have we gone through the effort of cleaning and kashering our homes? Have we done what the Holiday demands of us? Have we internalized and remembered the lessons of slavery and freedom? Have we remembered to feed the hungry? Have we remembered to welcome the stranger? Have we remembered to praise and to thank God?

If we've done all this, if Elijah sees this when he comes to our homes, then we have given him reason to stay. We have given him a reason to usher in the Messianic Age. If we've done all this, then we believe God will do His part in bringing peace and justice to the world. As difficult as the Pesach preparations are, they are infinitesimally much less difficult than bringing peace to the world. Let us do our part in this world, believing and knowing that God will do His part, the more difficult part. All it takes is a little effort to bring about great reward.

WHAT IS HANUKKAH? 8

When it comes to Hanukkah, the Talmud asks but one question - Mai Hanukkah? What is Hanukkah? While not necessarily rising to the level of the four questions we ask at the Seder, I would like to ask three questions. How do we celebrate Hanukkah? What isn't Hanukkah? And most importantly, Why is this holiday different from all the others?

The first question is how do we celebrate Hanukkah? Although the obvious answer is we do so by lighting a menorah (technically, a Hanukkiah), the truth is that Hanukkah is a holiday that can be celebrated in many different ways because it's not a Yom Tov, because of its relative lack of ritual, and because it lasts for eight days. While the High Holidays are celebrated in the synagogue, and Passover is celebrated in the home with a ritual meal, Hanukkah is celebrated either in the home, in the synagogue, or in any other place a Jew feels compelled or moved to do so. I have celebrated Hanukkah with a dinner dance at the synagogue, on Christmas Eve at a friend's

Hanukkah party, complete with the singing of Hanukkah carols, one year with cousins who I hadn't seen in about eighteen years, and even on a congregational cruise.

A friend's daughter spent one Hanukkah in Scotland. She brought her menorah, lit it, and even made latkes there. She said it didn't make her feel uncomfortable doing so despite the relatively few menorahs in the windows and the greater number of Christmas decorations. Once, through the magic of the internet, skype and webcams, I watched a friend light her Hanukkah candles in Israel.

Israel is an interesting place to celebrate Hanukkah. This same friend said, "As with all the holidays there, it's amazing to be celebrating the same occasion as everyone else. You see sufganiyot everywhere instead of candy canes, and many people have Hanukkah parties or make it a point to light candles together." She added, "And it's not so commercial. What is Hanukkah about in Israel? The culture, the songs, the history, the traditions of lighting candles and eating oil-filled food."

Speaking of Israel, my son spent Hanukkah there while on the Birthright program. He actually called one night (another true Hanukah miracle!) at around 8:15 in the evening our time. That made it after 3 am in Israel. He was out and about in Tel Aviv. I asked him how it felt to celebrate Hanukkah and Christmas in Israel. He said that Hanukkah was just a normal time, just a couple of menorahs around. And no Christmas at all.

It meant no songs on the radio, not being bombarded with holiday messages, no sales, and shopping sprees. In Israel, Hanukkah isn't about commercialism. It's celebrated for what it really is, a great and inspiring military victory. In the words of my friend's husband, a native Israeli, "Why do we celebrate Hanukkah? Because the Maccabees kicked butt!"

The second question is what Hanukkah is not about. Hanukkah is not about gifts, and it's not about competing with Christmas. Hanukkah is not a Jewish Christmas. My daughter, when she taught Hebrew School, had one student whose family celebrated Christmas, complete with a Christmas tree. They decorated their house with Christmas decorations. Okay, you might say, it happens in this day and age, especially if one of the parents is not Jewish. But in this case Both parents were Jewish. The child is being raised Jewish. Yet they celebrate Christmas.

The third and final question is "Why is Hanukkah different from all other holidays?" Another time, my son called me from school at around eleven pm. For my son to call in the first place is unusual; for him to call that late meant that something was wrong. He called because his roommate's parents were over and they were discussing what the most important Jewish holiday is. The parents said it was Yom Kippur. My son said it was Shabbat. They called the rabbi for the right answer. I said Purim because it will still be observed when the Mashiach comes. I figured that would throw them for a loop.

However, in thinking seriously about the most important Jewish holiday, my answer is Hanukkah because despite how they might celebrate it in Scotland or in Israel, for us in America, we can truly appreciate the original meaning of Hanukkah. Hanukkah is important because it is all about religious freedom. It is all about being proud of who we are as Jews.

Unfortunately, the great irony is that the Maccabees fought their battles because of the widespread assimilation of the Jewish people in their day. Today we celebrate their successful fight by being Hellenized ourselves, by being Americanized, by celebrating Christmas and the holiday season. Hanukkah - it's a Jewish Christmas - nothing more and nothing less. It's an opportunity to give gifts and have a party. We have forgotten the reason for the party.

We should party. We should celebrate being Jewish more often. However, what we should be celebrating is that we have a culture and a heritage that's worth fighting for. We should celebrate and be thankful that we live in a country where we can publicly proclaim that we are Jews, and not feel scared, embarrassed, or ashamed to do so. How many of our parents or grandparents were able to say that?

We live in a country where we make-up approximately 1.7% of the population. Yet we live in a country where approximately eight per cent of Congress is Jewish. We live in a country where there is a Menorah lighting ceremony at the White House, where the President of the United States publicly acknowledges the holiday and traditions of our people, and where there is a national menorah in Washington, D.C. And we live in a country where we feel no shame or reluctance to hold public menorah lighting ceremonies, where we can demonstrate the symbols of our faith, and where we proudly place our menorahs in the window so everyone can see.

What really lies at the heart of Hanukkah, for all its stories about war and miracles and oil, is that for the first and only time in our history, we fought a war for the right to practice our religion, observe the Torah, and preserve our values. We fought a war to ensure our religious freedom.

This is the message of Hanukkah. It's not about the season. It's not about Christmas. Here in America we commemorate and observe Hanukkah as the obligation to preserve our religious freedom by standing up as Jews for our own unique and special traditions and beliefs, and not merely as uninvited spectators at someone else's party.

Hanukkah is not a minor holiday. Hanukkah comes around once a year to remind us about the beauty of Jewish culture and about the dangers of assimilation. Many years ago a small group of fighters fought for the preservation of that culture and that religion. They succeeded. We face the same challenge and struggle today. Hopefully we too will succeed.

HEROES AND VILLAINS 9

It seems that in each and every generation, including our own, there is always a Haman, always a Hitler, always a Hamas, a Hezbollah or a Hussein, who want to destroy, not just Israel, but the entire Jewish people. It's interesting to note that each of these enemies begin with the letter "H." That is "H" as in HATE! Face it; we are just not treated like everybody else. No matter what; no matter where. Even those who don't exactly "hate" us, still don't exactly love us. That has been our story throughout history.

How do we respond to this hate? One way is based on our requirement to "Zachor;" to remember; to "Never Forget." We must always remember our past and use it as a reminder of how things can change for us at a moment's notice. At the same time, while we remember that past, as well as those who hate us and who have continuously sought to harm us, we must also remember and extol those in our history who, while living in dangerous times and circumstances, rose up to the occasion, and in turn saved the Jewish people. We must therefore not only remember "Hate," we must also remember another "H" word; "Heroes." There are plenty of examples throughout our history; examples of Jews, assimilated ones at that, who never lost sight of their Jewish identity, and made it their business to stand up for the Jewish people. We should remind ourselves that our history isn't only about Haman and Hitler, but about good, decent, God-fearing people, Jew and non-Jew alike, who have paved the way for us today.

The first such hero to emulate is Joseph. When we examine Joseph's tenure as prime minister of Egypt we learn rather quickly that he was very much a part of the fabric of Egyptian life and society, even though everyone knew he was Jewish and not an Egyptian. Because he dressed like an Egyptian and had an Egyptian name which befit his title, he fit in. Joseph looked and acted so Egyptian that his brothers didn't even recognize him when they saw him the first time!

Somehow, Joseph managed to lead a double life by also maintaining his Jewish identity. He gave his children Hebrew names and identities - Manasseh and Ephraim - raising them as Hebrews, while at the same time living in 'exile' and rising to the heights of political power. Yes, Joseph saved Egypt from a famine. More importantly, he saved his own family. Despite his personal animosity, he made it his business to make sure that his family, his brothers and their families, were taken care of in the land of Goshen.

Second is Queen Esther. Esther is considered one of the greatest of our heroes and heroines. Yet Esther didn't use her Hebrew name, Hadassah, and she obviously didn't appear to be Jewish, because neither the King nor Haman were aware of that fact. Like Joseph, Esther saved the Jewish people from extermination. Esther turned the King against Haman just like Joseph fed his brothers and their families in the time of famine. As great as their successes were, and the amount of compromises of their identity that were necessary, neither Joseph nor Esther ever lost their Jewish identity and their connection with their people. When push came to shove, they both revealed themselves for who they really were and saved the Jewish people.

There is another way of being a hero other than saving the Jewish people as evidenced by the Maccabees. The Maccabees were different in that they fought to save the Jewish religion - God and Torah - as opposed to saving the Jewish people. This was because the Greeks represented no threat to our physical existence, only to our religious existence. The Maccabees therefore had to protect Jewish observance, something which neither Joseph nor Esther had any need to do or inclination towards doing.

We need more Joseph's, Jews in positions of influence, who remember who they are, where they came from, and who never forget their "family." We need to remember Esther and Mordechai's battle to save the Jewish people and use it as inspiration and guidance for our continuing battle against those who hate us today. We need to remember that the Maccabees fought for the principle that a Jewish way of life is a life worth fighting for. Our task is to teach the lessons of these stories, of our heroes, to a new generation of Jews; to show them what it means to be a Jew and what it means to stand up to those who hate us.

This is why, in our time, whenever we mourn the loss of six million of our fellow Jews in the Holocaust, we should also be grateful to, be thankful for, and remember, those Heroes, who risked their lives to save Jews. Not only well known people like Oskar Schindler and the Bielski brothers, who saved hundreds if not thousands, but also lesser known heroes like Lubertus and Geeske te Kiefte, who risked their lives to save only a few, in Holland, during the Holocaust. We must focus on the good, the lives that were saved and the lives they spawned, each and every time we also think of the bad and the hate.

In the book, "A Night with the King," a modern Midrash on Megillat Esther, there is a line which reads, "Visibility, not assimilation, was the key to Jewish survival in this new land." Visibility! We as Jews have to remain visible, we have to remain vigilant, and we have to remember to emulate our heroes, and not just vilify our enemies.

Think of the message that would send! Judaism is about doing good and about recognizing those who do good. It is not only about remembering the evil and those who perpetrated it. A Judaism which is only about remembering our enemies, in the end, is not a Judaism worth fighting for. But a Judaism which reminds us about the sacrifices and heroic measures taken by our ancestors long ago, as well as by many heroes still today, including those who defend the land of Israel, is a Judaism which is always worth fighting for and preserving.

PART IV
ETHICS AND VALUES

SPIRIT 1

F or Moses, a man who was slow of speech and a reluctant leader and messenger, appearing time and again before Pharaoh, urging him to "Let My People Go," must have been very draining. One would think therefore that Moses would have asked for and received some help from his people, from the Israelites, especially from the elders. After all, when God first appeared to Moses at the burning bush, He told Moses to approach the elders with the message that God has heard their cries and is about to free them from their bondage.

But when Moses approached the Israelites with this piece of good news that God will soon be freeing them, delivering them, redeeming them, taking them, and bringing them back home to the Promised Land, the Torah tells us, plainly and to the point, that they would not listen to Moses. The Israelites turned their back on Moses. They offered him no help with his mission. If Moses wanted to go to Pharaoh, if he wanted to bring a few plagues, if he wanted to liberate the Israelites, he'd just have to do it alone. They were not going to help. They were not going to get involved.

Why not? Because they suffered from two maladies, "Mikotzer ruach u'me'avodah kashah." The second term, "Avodah Kashah," is easy to explain. It literally means hard work. We understand how the Israelites' hard work, their slavery, would make them tired and exhausted. Even if they could believe in Moses' message of liberation, they were in no physical condition to do anything about it. To put it another way, they had no strength. We can certainly understand why it was too difficult for them to make the many trips from Goshen to Pharaoh's palace.

Doesn't that happen to us as well? We get tired after a long day or week of work. We look forward to the weekend; to relax; to get time off. It's a basic human need. We were not created to work twenty four hours a day, seven days a week. For that matter neither was God. He too took a day off to rest.

The more important term, as well as the more difficult term to understand is "Kotzer Ruach." The Etz Hayim Chumash translates "Kotzer Ruach" as "Their spirit crushed." Rashi understands the term to mean shortness of breath. Rabbi Samson Raphael Hirsch translates "Kotzer Ruach" as "impatience." It's a term capable of multiple meanings.

Nahum Sarna however translates "kotzer ruach" as shortness of spirit. Sarna explains that the Israelites had little spirit left in them. They had no more emotional or psychological energy left, and hence, no more fight. They had become so conditioned to slavery, that they were emotionally numb to the potential for freedom; psychologically incapable of accepting the challenge Moses placed in front of them. The Israelites did not listen to Moses, did not offer to help or get involved, because of an emotional, rather than a physical, inability to understand their current situation and to realize that they in fact had a hope, a future, and a destiny as a nation. Kotzer ruach led the Israelites to refuse freedom, refuse nationhood, refuse a land they could call their own, and refuse a future for their children.

Thus, while avodah kashah is physical weariness, kotzer ruach is emotional and spiritual weariness. While avodah kashah means that the body has given up, kotzer ruach means that the spirit has given up. Kotzer ruach occurs when the dark reality of the present overpowers all dreams for the future. It explains why we resist change, even when change will create an improved lifestyle. It explains why we resign ourselves to living in a bad situation only because we don't have the strength to change the circumstances of our lives.

Kotzer ruach is a bad condition but it is a part of human life. We all go through it at various times. Some more than others. Yes, it's a syndrome, a malady, that was named by God Himself, not some modern day psychologist, but it's a condition that we all can and must overcome.

Today, we as a people, also experience kotzer ruach. We are so beaten down by terrorist attacks, by the surge in anti-Semitism, by the constant anti-Israel reports in the media, that we've become immune or resigned to them. Many of us just give up, rather than get involved and fight back. However, like Moses, who refused to give in to this malady, fortunately for us today, we have many leaders, across all walks of Jewish life, who also fight back against the kotzer ruach that plagues the rest of us. Fortunately, there are not just leaders, but ordinary Jews, of all walks of life, who don't let the bad news get to them, who don't let the problems we are facing and the continuing uphill battle we face, stop them from getting involved, from speaking out and acting out. They are examples of how we must fight against becoming kotzer ruach ourselves.

"Kotzer Ruach" came before "Avodah Kasha" to remind us that only when our spirit was restored, when we were emotionally and psychologically ready for the fight, a process which did not happen overnight, but over time, after witnessing the ten plagues, that we had the physical strength to finally pack up and leave Egypt.

There is a lesson for us in these words. It is the importance of spirit to our lives. It is the importance of not living with a broken spirit. It is the importance of realizing that just as the spirit isn't broken overnight, so too it can't be restored overnight either. It takes time, but it's something we should consider devoting time to.

A broken spirit can always be restored, whether it's our own, a loved one's, or a friend's or a neighbor's. We should maintain a positive outlook, realizing that the spirit comes first. Then, if the mind is willing, if the spirit is willing, the body will follow.

We really can't lead full, happy and productive lives if we have kotzer ruach, but we can if we are maleh ruach; if we are full of spirit. If we lead our lives by constantly focusing on all that is wrong with our lives, or on all that is wrong with the world, it will inevitably lead to kotzer ruach. However, if we focus on what is right in our lives and in the world, that is living maleh ruach.

We can't think for a minute that we're too old, we're too sick, or there's just nothing we can do about a situation or a problem. That is kotzer ruach. Rather, we must believe that there is always more we can yet accomplish; for ourselves, our loved ones', our community, the Jewish people, and yes, even the world. That is living a life that is maleh ruach.

Ruach is joy. Ruach is hope. Ruach is optimism. Kotzer ruach is the opposite. Which would you rather have in your lives? Remember, at the age of eighty, Moses was still climbing mountains!

Every day, in the birchot hashachar, the blessings with which we begin each morning service, we thank God as "Hanotein layaef koach," "He who gives the weary strength." Every day we are tired, whether spiritually or physically, but every day we thank God for giving us new strength, and then live that day with that strength.

Every day let us stop, whether it's at the synagogue or from the comfort of our homes, and take a moment to appreciate and take advantage of the renewed strength that God has given us. And let us resolve to live each day, maleh ruach - with, and full, of ruach.

PRICELESS 2

W e've all seen those Visa commercials; the ones which place a price tag on various items but in the end refer to the one thing in life which has no price, which is priceless, like lifting the Stanley Cup. It's a great concept. Judaism even has its own Visa. Only we don't call it Visa. We call it Mitzvah! Mitzvahs are truly priceless. No matter how you look at it, Mitzvah is what Judaism is really all about.

We are all commanded to perform mitzvahs. In fact mitzvah means commandment, not just a good deed. Nevertheless we often feel as though we need a reason to do them; a reward, if you will, for going out of our way to perform mitzvahs for others. One reason, from Chabad philosophy, tells us that the more mitzvahs we perform the sooner the Mashiach will come. Another reason tells us that the more mitzvahs we perform, the more mitzvah points we accumulate; and the more mitzvah points we accumulate, the more likely it is we will receive a share in the Olam Haba, the next world, or the Garden of Eden as it were.

Then again, if mitzvahs are truly priceless, we shouldn't need a reason to perform them. We just do them even if there is no reward; whether it's a thank you from the person you are helping, hastening the coming of the Mashiach, or securing a place in the World to come.

There is one incident in the Torah, one small mitzvah if you will, which speaks volumes as to the character of the Jewish people, and about their willingness to perform a mitzvah, even in the midst of all their grumbling and complaining about everything and anything. Despite all the hesitations which were expressed about leaving Egypt, about crossing the Red Sea, and about surviving in the wilderness, Moses and the Jewish people performed one simple task which demonstrated why they were worthy of being the chosen people. A simple task, a mitzvah, one might call priceless.

As Joseph was about to die, he made his brothers promise to take his remains back with them to Israel for burial there. Just as Joseph made sure to bury his father Jacob in Israel, Joseph wanted to ensure that he too would be buried in Israel. Two hundred and ten years later the Israelites were finally ready to leave Egypt. Certainly all of Joseph's brothers who had made that pledge had died. But now that the time to fulfill that promise had arrived, who would fulfill that promise? Was the promise binding on the third and fourth generations? Were they even aware of the promise? The answer is yes! Moses was aware. He knew that it was his responsibility to make sure this promise was carried out. As the Israelites left Egypt, Moses took the bones of Joseph with him.

If Moses had forgotten this promise nobody would have noticed; nobody would have cared. Moses, however, remembered and he cared. He made sure, that while the rest of the Israelites were packing their meager belongings, and collecting gold and silver from their Egyptian neighbors, he would go out of his way to fulfill a promise, to do a mitzvah.

Moses wasn't thinking about the Mashiach. He wasn't thinking about the World to Come. He wasn't expecting any kind of thank you note from Joseph's family. He wasn't even expecting to be named Jew of the Year and get a plaque or some other memento for his efforts. Moses performed this mitzvah, fulfilled an old promise, merely for its own sake, without any thought or expectation of reward. There's a word for that. Priceless.

Moses teaches us the essence of what it means to do a mitzvah; of what it means to be Jewish. We should perform mitzvot for their own sake, to help others, to do good for others, without any expectation of reward. If we expect a reward, if we expect platitudes for our supposedly selfless and good natured actions, and we don't get them, then we stop doing them. The worst thing that can happen is that we stop doing mitzvot. On the other hand, if we do mitzvot purely for their own sake, without any expectation of reward, or honor, or thanks, and if we aren't so rewarded, honored or thanked, then we won't be bothered or annoyed. We won't be disappointed. It won't hinder us from doing more mitzvot in the future.

It's nice to be thanked, to be acknowledged, to be appreciated, and to be recognized, for doing something good, whether it's a mitzvah, a mere good deed, something at work, or anything we may do for another. Psychologically, we want to think that the more encouragement, the more positive reinforcement we get, the more it will encourage us and lead us to do more. But Judaism reminds us time and again that it's not about the reward. It's about doing the mitzvot, large and small, which help others. That is what counts and that is what we should never stop doing even if our efforts aren't appreciated.

Moses wasn't thanked for his tireless efforts in bringing back the bones of Joseph for burial, but that didn't stop Moses from continuing to do mitzvot for his people. The lesson is clear. We do mitzvot because we are commanded to do them and because we help people, and not for any expectation of reward.

But sometimes there are rewards. Just as Moses took care to bring back Joseph's bones, even though he was not obligated to do so, God Himself took care to personally see to Moses' burial. Moses however wasn't the only one who was rewarded. Moses' action set an example for the rest of the Israelites, who carried Joseph's casket with them throughout their forty years of wandering in the desert before burying it in Shechem. The Book of Joshua says that the "Children of Israel," the people as a whole, were given the credit for seeing to the proper burial of Joseph. A great reward for a small task. In other words, priceless.

Moses isn't the only one who does mitzvahs. So can we. A friend shared the story of how she helped a woman who had accidentally locked her keys, wallet and phone in her car. She offered the woman her phone to call AAA. Later, my friend was at the register of a store and couldn't read a label. The cashier let her use his glasses, and the woman behind her gave her one of her coupons.

As we say, "Mitzvah goreret mitzvah," one mitzvah leads to another. This is how we should perform mitzvot. Not by thinking of the reward, not by expecting thanks, but by doing them for their own sake, and for the influence they may have on others who will hopefully emulate our behavior by doing their own mitzot.

ONE SMALL STEP FOR MAN

3

On July 20, 1969 most of the world was sitting glued to their television sets watching Neil Armstrong set foot on the moon. We were stunned and amazed that in our lifetime we would actually see man walk on the moon; amazed not only that it could happen, but that we'd even have something called a television set on which to witness it live. When Neil Armstrong first set foot on the moon, he uttered those memorable words, "That's one small step for man, one giant leap for mankind."

Did you ever really stop and think about those words, what they mean in a larger context than just man setting foot on the moon? Did you ever stop and think about what it took to get there, to reach that faraway place? As much as we might like to think of it happening this way, Apollo 11 didn't just happen overnight. Starting with President Kennedy's clarion call in 1961 that we will send a man to the moon before the end of the decade, it took over eight years for that dream to actually come true. While to some, especially looking back on that time some forty years later, those eight years seem like eight seconds, the truth is, that a lot of effort went into putting that first man on the moon.

There were literally thousands of people over the years who worked on the Apollo project, anonymous people who worked for NASA and for the aerospace industry. There were countless hours of pain-staking labor, of trial and error, of building and rebuilding, of tests and re-tests, in order to get it right. There were other space missions that preceded Apollo 11, including the ill-fated Apollo 1, where three astronauts died in a cabin fire.

We don't think about those things though. We don't think of the many small steps that had to be taken by many men, in order for us to get where we wanted to go. We only seem to recall that one giant leap, the final step, the reaching of the ultimate goal. We remember that it was Neil Armstrong who was the first man to set foot on the moon. By a quirk of history and fate, he was the one who was at the right place at the right time for this historic moment.

There are a number of similarities between what happened to the Israelites in the desert and the Apollo story because the Torah, like the Apollo space program, is also about getting man to reach a particular destination. The Torah actually gives us two destinations. The first is a physical destination; reaching the land of Israel. The second is a spiritual destination; becoming closer to God and better people by observing God's commandments.

Man could not have reached the moon without all the effort and manpower of so many. So too, the Israelites journey through the desert to reach the Promised Land could not have been possible without the efforts not only of Moses and Aaron, but like the Apollo program, through the manpower, trial and error, and even death, of so many others. It was only through these efforts, that the Israelites were able to reach their destination; the Promised Land.

In the third month following the Exodus from Egypt, the Israelites received the Ten Commandments. In a way it was a call, a clarion call for the people to move forward to their next and ultimate goal - conquering the Land of Canaan. Like Kennedy's call for man to land on the moon, this journey did not happen overnight. It took forty years, because of what happened to the Israelites in the desert.

In the desert we saw the realities and practicalities of life. We read about politics, war, rebellion, gossip, and of all the other problems which arise in any community and society. We realized that life isn't always some pipe dream about man walking on the moon, or immediately entering the Promised Land, but involves real world problems, both domestic and foreign, which stood in the way of immediately realizing this dream.

Look at how the Torah addresses these real world, practical problems. It teaches us that only by dealing with these small problems, can the bigger problems get solved and the lofty goals reached. Among the many issues which the Israelites needed to resolve before conquering Canaan, was who would get what piece of land. The law was very simple at the time. Property belonged to the man and when he died his property, including his share of land, was inherited by his sons. Daughters? Forget about it! Well at least until the daughters of Zelophehad showed up.

Zelophehad was a member of the tribe of Manasseh, who died leaving behind five daughters and no sons. Under the biblical laws of inheritance, these women would be left with nothing. They then took the unusual step of appearing before Moses to argue that the law was unjust and needed to be changed. Moses asked God what to do. God replied, in no uncertain terms, that the daughters were right. From now on the rule would be that if a man died without leaving sons, his property would go to his daughters.

However, this new law led to another problem. Members of the tribe of Manasseh rightly complained that if these five women were to marry men from any of the other tribes, then their sons will inherit not only their own father's land, but Zelophehad's land as well. This would lead to the unfair result of having people from other tribes owning land that belongs to the tribe of Manasseh. If this were to happen, the total amount of land belonging to Manasseh would be permanently reduced.

Good point! Moses thought about it and then issued another new rule. The daughters may inherit under the old rule, but only if they marry members of their own tribe. If they marry members of a different tribe, they may not inherit.

Okay, problem solved. We're ready to move on. This was exactly how things happened and progressed. We encountered problems and we solved them. We learned that nothing is ever problem free; not putting a man on the moon, and not entering the Promised Land.

There is one important difference between these two events, the difference which makes the Torah so special, and such a lasting guide for human behavior. If asked to name the members of the Apollo 11 crew, most likely our memory starts to fade after Neil Armstrong. That is why the Torah goes out of its way to tell us the names of the daughters of Zelophehad; Machlah, Tirzah, Hoglah, Milcah and Noah. We tend to forget people and their names. However we must never forget the people, large and small, who enabled us to reach our destinations; the people who helped shape our laws and society. These five women were named to also remind us that women, even in Biblical times, deserved recognition. These five women are specifically mentioned in order to impress upon us the important lesson that every person who is involved in making our society better, or more just, is deserving of recognition.

We weren't alive thirty five hundred years ago to witness the events that were described in the Torah. Many of us were alive, however, and can recall, the miraculous events of forty years ago, when man achieved the impossible and walked on the moon. What we can take away from both historical events is that there are many small steps that need to be taken by man in order to make that one giant leap for mankind. We can't just snap our fingers and like magic walk on the moon or conquer Canaan. It took a long time to get to both places with many steps and missteps along the way.

We still have many more goals to achieve; many more moons to conquer. We still have many more societal ills left to eradicate; more tikkun olam yet to accomplish. If we are patient, if we allow ourselves to take those small steps, and if we recognize the efforts and sacrifices of all those who helped us get there, then we too will be able to make what hopefully will be many more giant leaps for mankind.

REQUEST, NOT DEMAND 4

Recalling all the strife, dissension and rebellion which we read about in the Book of Numbers, one thing stands out. They were all caused by.... Words! Korach spoke out against God and His appointed leader, Moses; the spies spoke out against the Land of Israel; Miriam was stricken with leprosy because she spoke out against Moses. All of these problems occurred because of what the instigators had been saying. They used their words to make demands and to incite the people. Their words got them in trouble; it led them to selfish and destructive behavior.

Now contrast those words, those demands, with another incident in the Torah. Following the war against Midian there were many spoils to divide among the people, including 675,000 sheep, 372,000 cattle, and 61,000 asses. How they were able to count so accurately is a story for another day. They must have had a good bookkeeper!

Given what we know of the Israelites in the desert, being stubborn and stiff necked, and using every excuse they could think of for personal gain, you would think the soldiers would keep what they could. Instead they made a full accounting and divided the booty according to what God devised, giving 1/1000 to God, some to the Levites, and some to the soldiers themselves. No dissension. No squabbling over who deserves what or how much. In fact, the commanders even approached Moses and gave all that they had collected as an offering to God.

Immediately afterward, we are told that the tribes of Reuben, Gad and Manasseh wanted to stay on the Eastern side of the Jordan River because it had better grazing land for their abundant cattle. They didn't just say we are staying here. They didn't just claim the land for themselves and be done with everyone else. They went to Moses and calmly pleaded their case. They approached Moses, explained their situation, and made their request. Moses immediately believed that their desire was to avoid having to fight to conquer the Land of Canaan, but the tribes immediately refuted that notion, saying that their request had nothing to do with avoiding their responsibility to the other tribes. To prove this, they were willing to be the first in battle. They would act as shock troops and they made a solemn vow to do just that.

Imagine that! A real dialogue took place. No threats; no rebellion. Just a legitimate request presented in a calm, non-threatening manner. What followed was not a plague or punishment or death or destruction. What followed was an agreement; a meeting of the minds between the parties. Strife was avoided.

This sudden change of mind and heart, this sudden change of tone came about because of what was discussed in the previous chapter; the request from the daughters of Zelophehad to inherit their father's land. When faced with this request, Moses didn't know what to do, not only because he wasn't told of this possibility on Mount Sinai, but because for the first time, he was actually approached by someone in a non-threatening, non-confrontational manner. For the first time, Moses was actually asked for permission to do something. Not yelled at; not threatened; but asked nicely and politely to fulfill a certain need.

This is why, in response to Moses' inquiry, God answered, "Ken b'not Zelophehad dovrot." While that phrase can be translated as "The plea of Zelophehad's daughters is just," I prefer to translate it as "Yes, look at how Zelophehad's daughters speak."

This is how we are supposed to speak. We should make proper requests, in the proper tone of voice, and not make threats or unreasonable demands. Maybe when the Israelites witnessed the success of Zelophehad's daughters and contrasted that to the utter failure of Korach, they learned an important lesson. They learned how to speak and the importance of words. They understood and took to heart the dangers of idle threats and rash behavior.

The earlier generation, the one which had known slavery, was used to being spoken to in a certain way, the way of the Egyptian slave master, or the way of an all powerful God, or by necessity a strong leader. This new generation not only needed to be spoken to differently, they also needed to learn for themselves how to speak, both with each other and with its leaders. Having witnessed the behavior of Zelophehad's daughters, they finally understood. From then on, although there were still disagreements, as there always will be in any community or any institution, these disagreements did not lead to strife and dissension, but were handled in a mature, respectful, mutually amenable way.

The Israelites learned a lesson which we should take to heart today as well. There is a way of talking to people, and there is a way of not talking to people. There is a way of getting your point across, making a request, and getting a positive response, and there is a way of not doing so. That was the lesson the Israelites seemed to have finally learned; to be mindful and respectful of how we speak to others, how we make requests and not demands of others, how we express our appreciation and gratitude, and how we can "always catch more flies with honey than with vinegar."

SELFLESSNESS   5

W hy do we have laws and rituals? By the same token, why do we study ancient laws and rituals from the Torah which no longer apply to our everyday lives? The answer is that our laws and rituals, whether we are still able to practice them or not, exist to teach us values and ethics in how we should live our everyday lives today. A perfect example of this is the law of bikkurim, the law of the first fruits. If we were farmers during biblical times we would know how important our first fruits would have been. It would have been a harbinger of the crops to come. It would have showed that our hard work and efforts have paid off. It would have provided food for our family. We could have used the extra fruits to trade with our neighbors for other crops that we needed.

But not so fast says the Torah! The law of bikkurim, tells us that we must take our first fruits and.... give them to the Kohen. We must give away what we've worked so hard for; what we've waited for; what we relied on for our sustenance. How can God command such a thing if we need to rely on the land and our crops for our very survival? We want and need them for ourselves. But Judaism wants us to behave and act differently and the law of the first fruits exists to teach us precisely how to behave.

The farmer who worked so hard to produce his crop received his reward when those first fruits appeared. He then tied a red ribbon around them to identify them as his. When the fruits reached maturity he would pack them into a basket and bring them to the Temple to give to the Kohen. When he did, he wouldn't just bring the basket to the door of the Kohen's house, ring the bell, and run away, like a reverse trick or treat. If he were to do so, can you imagine the Kohen's surprise when he woke up in the morning and found all these baskets on his front porch? Instead the farmer, the Israelite, had to appear in front of the Kohen and recite a particular formula.

Why go through all this ritual? Because this act reinforced the value of generosity. After investing so much effort in producing these first fruits, the farmer valued them and felt attached to them. However, when he brought his fruits to the Kohen, that act of giving strengthened his sense of generosity. As Maimonides commented, this act existed to "Strengthen the trait of generosity and to reduce the lust for food and acquisition of wealth." He could have, he would have, he wanted to, eat these fruits himself. But the act of giving it away teaches us to curb our appetites and our pursuit of material goods, because they are not always ours to keep.

The ability to recognize and be thankful for the good that is bestowed upon us, thanking God, is another value that is strengthened by performing this particular ritual. Through this commandment, through this act of bringing the first fruits to the Kohen, we acknowledged that it is not solely through our own efforts we obtained this bounty. Rather, everything was, and still is, by the will of God.

Unlike the sacrifices, which were offered to God, and whose purpose was to bring us closer to God, the offering of the first fruits was not to God, but to man. This teaches us that not only must we rely on God, but also on each other; that our fruits come about not just through our own hands, but with the help of others. Therefore we must be willing to share with others, especially the Kohens and Levis, or any-one else, the poor especially, who didn't have crops of their own, but who had to rely on the people's generosity to sustain them.

When we brought the fruits to the Kohen we recited a line from the Passover Haggadah. It was the history of Israel before we became a people, going back to the time when "My father was a wandering Aramean," and to our slavery in Egypt. We recited this passage because only someone who has experi-enced hardship knows that nothing is to be taken for granted. In order to feel grateful for one's current condition, the hard-ships of the past must be recalled so we do not become com-placent or forget those who are still suffering.

After we brought our fruits to the Kohen, and after we recited that particular piece of our history, we were commanded to do something else. "And you shall enjoy, together with the Levite and the stranger in your midst, all the bounty that the Lord your God has bestowed upon you and your household." We are commanded, actually commanded, to rejoice. We are commanded to be glad that we have shared our first fruits with those who are less fortunate. We are commanded not to be stingy or resentful, but to actually be happy that others get to share in our bounty as well.

In our selfishness, we want to keep what is ours and only share it with those close to us. However, we are commanded to share it with others; with the Levite who has no land and no fruit of his own, and even with the stranger. How much against human nature is that?

We must also rejoice when we do so. We should be happy and grateful that we have the ability to share with others; those less fortunate and those we don't even know. If we stop and think about it, isn't this something to make us proud? To be able to share with others? Even if the Torah didn't command it wouldn't you feel a smile creeping on your face when you do?

Our society places great emphasis on achieving happiness and on accumulating the means to do so. These things however don't really bring us happiness. They are temporary; they're not real. That is why we say, "The best things in life are free," and "You can't take it with you." True happiness, permanent happiness, comes from being less selfish. It comes from doing for others. Our society's definition of happiness is a way of escaping from reality, but Judaism's definition of happiness is a way to connect to a different reality. The reality of God, and of selflessness. The reality of the good that is in each and every one of us.

Selfishness is a mirror. It blinds us. It doesn't allow us to see the other side; to see life. It doesn't permit us to see that we have to help others and the good that can come out of it if we do. While we no longer bring our first fruits to the Kohen, we can nonetheless bring the first of our efforts to help others; to be less selfish; to be more generous; to be more grateful. Most importantly we should truly rejoice in what we do for others.

WINNING ISN'T EVERYTHING

6

The level of civility in our public discourse, in campaigns, among our elected leaders, in fact in all walks of life, has descended to unconscionably low levels. Bill Clinton called it "The politics of personal destruction." He would know as he was certainly the victim of some of it. The name of the game is to destroy the other person, any person, for any reason, or no reason whatsoever. Some people get a perverse thrill out of putting people down, out of slandering and embarrassing their opponent, especially when they don't get their way. Rather than engaging in a legitimate debate of the issues, rather than accepting the fact that sometimes your view, your position, your candidate, is in the minority, some people lash out and engage in negative campaigns, and negative attacks, whose only goal is to put down the other side.

This is not the way our leaders did things, which is why we should examine the example they set for us. After over forty years of leadership of the Jewish people Moses was about to die and turn over his leadership to Joshua. Moses was certainly disappointed that he was not permitted to lead the Israelites the Promised Land, his lifetime wish and goal. He called Joshua to take over for him after he is gone and he strengthened Joshua with inspiring words.

Moses did this without displaying any sense of bitterness or jealousy towards Joshua, although he must have been somewhat envious of Joshua's new role. Moses didn't just walk away. He did so gracefully and graciously. He helped Joshua assume the mantle of leadership. He gave him advice and made the transition easier. He didn't sulk or take his ball and go home. Moses handed over the leadership to Joshua with a "good eye," with even more enthusiasm than he had been commanded to give. He transferred the leadership with both hands even though God only told him to use one hand. Moses did not do anything to publically lower Joshua in the eyes of the people. Instead, he abided by God's decision and did not engage in the politics of personal destruction.

Moses taught us that competition is not healthy for one's character. If a person can only succeed by putting another down, then he becomes consumed with wishing the other to fail, rather than trying to succeed himself. For example, every sports team begins the season thinking and hoping that it will win the championship. Yet everyone knows that only one team will be left holding the trophy at the end of the year. Every other team will look back at the season as a failure because they didn't win.

We have created a society which preaches that if you are not the best, if you don't finish first, if another beats you, then you are not worth much; you are a failure. If the team doesn't win it fires the coach or the manager. The fans put the blame on them because someone has to take the blame. No one believes the old saying, "It's not whether you win or lose, it's how you play the game" anymore. Instead we believe that, "Winning isn't everything; it's the only thing."

We live in an environment which motivates through competition. If all I have to do to be successful is to beat you, it's a whole lot easier to cause you to do worse than me, rather than to get myself to do better than you. The result is that people will not push themselves to truly reach their personal best if all they have to do to flourish is defeat someone else.

Yes, we should be competitive, but only with ourselves. If I ran the mile in eight minutes last week, let me try to run it in seven minutes today. If I got a ninety on the last test, let me attempt to get a ninety five this time. If I got a raise at work, let me try for a bigger one next year. It should only matter what we do, not whether the next person ran faster, scored higher or received a bigger raise. Success is accomplished by struggling against ourselves, trying to improve upon our personal past performance, trying to better ourselves, in all that we do, but not ever at the expense of someone else. If I scored a ninety on the test instead of a ninety five, I shouldn't be resentful if my classmate scored that ninety five; I should be happy for him.

Competition and winning are not the most important goals in life. Rather, it's treating all people with respect that what's most important, while not basing or measuring our success on someone else's failures. While Moses taught us much during his lifetime, perhaps the most valuable lesson he might have passed down occurred at the end of his life when he taught us how not to engage in damaging rivalries and competitions, of not engaging in the politics of personal destruction, but of lifting up others, being happy for their successes, and most of all, that winning isn't everything.

Shh! - Simple, Haimish and Humble

7

If we want to make those proverbial New Year's resolutions, if we want to make changes in our lives, it is natural to ask ourselves, what do I change and how do I change. We might get overwhelmed by the answers because they might not be as simple as we first thought. We might even come up with a laundry list of negative character traits which we want to change; to improve on. We then look at that list and we take one of two possible courses of action. We either resolve to make all the changes on that "to do" list, or we see that it's way too long, we can never finish it, we give up, and throw that list away without even trying.

However, there is a third option. We can make a realistic list of only a few changes to work on. If we see that it's manageable and doable, if we succeed, then we can always add to that list in the future. In that vein, here are three simple, but related traits to work on; traits which are not only reachable and doable, but traits which will hopefully encourage you to continue the process of change.

These three traits are Simplicity, Haimishness, and Humility. Let us learn to live simply, let us learn to live more haimishly, and let us learn to live with humility.

The first trait is simplicity. Simplicity is one of the keys to a good life; the kind of life we pray for. A movie came out a few years ago called "A Serious Man." It showed how sometimes even what we perceive as simple really isn't so. It had a great quote, presumably from Rashi, which said, "Receive with simplicity everything that happens to you." What a great line. What great words to live by.

In our society simple has a negative connotation. We don't like simple. We want something more. Admit it, when you hear that a person is simple, don't you immediately assume that he's stupid? Think of the "Simple Son" at the Passover Seder. He is called "Tam." Yet "Tam" is an interesting word. It appears many times in the Bible but never with the negative connotation of being stupid. Rather in all the biblical examples, "tam" means wholehearted with God, or as with Abraham, blameless with God. It's not so simple then. What we call "simple" has a much more positive connotation in Judaism.

The word "tam" also means flavor or taste in Yiddish. Simply put, if you are tam, if you have tam, then you have flavor. You are simple only in the sense that you are humble and haimish. However you have something, many things even, going for you.

The Bible refers to Job as "Ish tam v'yashar yirei Adonai," a sincere and upright man, God-fearing and shunning evil." This is the true definition of simplicity. It is what we should all strive to be. Sincere. Upright. God fearing. The person who is simple is not perfect, because perfection is not a human possibility. The person who is simple still has room to grow and has a desire to grow. It is not easy, and it may not even be humanly possible to always be simple. However we have much growing and learning still to do and this should be our goal. So remember, in the words of Rashi, "Receive with simplicity everything that happens to you."

The next trait is haimishness. The dictionary defines haimish as Yiddish for "homey." This is not exactly the clearest of definitions, because, maybe, it's not capable of definition. As Supreme Court Justice Potter Stewart said in defining pornography... "I know it when I see it." Yes, that's haimish. We all know it when we see it, even if we can't really define it.

David Brooks, a Jewish columnist for the New York Times, wrote an op-ed piece he called "The Haimish Line." It might be perhaps the best definition of haimish there is. Brooks writes, "It's a Yiddish word that suggests warmth, domesticity and unpretentious conviviality." Brooks concludes with some good advice. "Buy experiences instead of things; buy many small pleasures instead of a few big ones; pay now for things you can look forward to and enjoy later. And sometimes it's best to spend carefully so you can stay south of the Haimish Line."

What great advice. What a perfect definition of Haimish. What a perfect guide for us to live haimishly. Let us focus on what is truly important in life. People. Friends. Family. Not wealth, status or possession. Let us resolve to live haimishly. Remember, in the words of Rashi, "To receive with haimishness everything that happens to you."

The final trait, and perhaps the most difficult to master is humility. The Torah tells us that "Moses was very humble, more than any person on the face of the Earth." Yet that begs the classic question. If Moses wrote down the words of the Torah, how is it possible for him to be humble after God tells him that he is the most humble man in the world? In other words, "I am the most humble man who ever lived. If I do say so myself!"

The answer lies in the definition of humility. A person with true humility is open to learning from others, and is not afraid of asking questions when he has doubts, or asking for help when needed. A person with true humility is also open to accepting constructive criticism. This is because a truly humble person doesn't have the need to feel more powerful than another, especially by putting that other person down. A truly humble person doesn't have to pick fights or arguments. Rather, he asks for forgiveness and doesn't place the blame on others. A truly humble person sees the good in everyone, and not the bad or the faults.

On the other hand, an arrogant person, one who does not demonstrate the trait of humility, demands that everything be done his way. The arrogant person has no patience for anyone other than himself. Wouldn't we rather be humble? Isn't it better to accept things even though they're not always the way we would like them to be? Aren't we better off focusing on the good and positive in each situation? Of course we are. This is why the humble person gets more joy out of life than the arrogant person.

God always speaks to us. Sometimes he speaks loudly and sometimes he speaks in a whisper. Whispers are done quietly. We say SHH!.....

It stands for ....
S-Simplicity
H-Haimishness
H- Humility
We should be open to change and to growth and we should be open to having a little more simplicity, haimishness, and humility in our lives, because the simple things, the haimish things, and the humble things, combine to make a complete life. Remember, in the words of Rashi, "To receive with simplicity, with haimishness, and with humility, everything that happens to you." Simple. Haimish. Humble. If we work on these traits, then other positive traits, kindness, compassion, caring, will certainly follow.

THE PERFECT GAME

8

In Brooklyn, New York, there is a school called Chush, which caters to learning disabled children. At a Chush dinner, the father of a Chush child delivered a speech, crying out, "Where is the perfection in my son Shaya? Everything God does is done with perfection. But my child cannot understand things as other children do. My child cannot remember facts and figures as other children do. Where is God's perfection?" I believe," the father answered, "That when God brings a child like this into the world, the perfection that he seeks is in the way people react to this child." He then related the now widely known story about how his son was allowed to play in a baseball game with other kids who let Shaya score the winning run and treated him like a hero. "That day," said the father softly with tears rolling down his face, "Those 18 boys reached their level of God's perfection."

What exactly does "Their level of God's perfection" mean? It might mean that God has a level of perfection that those boys managed to reach through their actions. Or it might mean that we each have our own "level of perfection," and that "level of perfection" might be different for each of us. However, the idea of perfection, or of us reaching God's perfection, is really a non-starter. This is because only God is perfect.

None of us who are human are perfect. We might try our best to achieve perfection but we don't always succeed. That's okay. God doesn't actually expect us to be perfect. Therefore, our level of God's perfection must be defined by how we react to, and deal with, not only our own imperfections, but the imperfections of others as well. What God does expect from us, and what God wants to know, is how we react when there is imperfection around us; even when it's through no fault of our own. This is because how we react to imperfection is the key to defining our own perfection. Maybe that's the true definition of perfection.

No person is perfect. Everyone makes mistakes. Some are easily forgivable and some are easily correctable. On the other hand, some mistakes can't be corrected and have a lasting impact on those whom they affected. What if we make a mistake and we can't correct it? What if the mistake we make is so big that it has a lasting impact on the people whom it affected, if not on history itself? What do we do then? How do we deal with it? Perhaps baseball can tell us how.

Just as in life, there are mistakes made in baseball. In baseball terms we call them errors. In the course of a baseball game most of these errors don't affect the outcome of the game, just like our human errors, often done on a daily basis, usually have no lasting effect on the course of our lives. Then there are those errors which do have a profound impact and effect on the course of our lives.

172

On June 2nd, 2010, Armando Galarraga, a pitcher for the Detroit Tigers, had retired twenty six consecutive Cleveland Indian batters. One more out and he would have thrown a perfect game, getting all twenty seven batters he faced, out. The next batter hit a ground ball to second base. The second baseman easily picked up the ball and threw to Galarraga, who was covering first base for the twenty seventh, and final out. The throw beat the runner, the out was made, and Galarraga would go down in baseball history as having thrown a perfect game.

But wait. Not so fast.

The umpire, Jim Joyce, inexplicably called the runner....... safe.

No perfect game; not even a no-hitter, and no going down in baseball history. All because of a mistake, maybe an honest mistake, but a mistake nonetheless, committed by the umpire. Calling the runner safe, when everyone in the stadium and millions watching on television, knew he was out, will probably haunt that umpire for the rest of his career.

What happened afterwards though, the way both Galarraga and Joyce acted afterwards is the way we should behave when a mistake is made, whether we are the one who made the mistake and need to apologize, or whether we are the one who has been the subject of the mistake. Joyce didn't downplay or even deny that he made a mistake. He admitted his error before he tearfully asked Galarraga for a chance to apologize. Galarraga readily accepted that sincere apology, saying, "He felt really bad. "He probably felt more bad than me." And then smiling, he added, "Nobody's perfect."

In Judaism, we call this teshuvah. Or atonement! It is the way we are supposed to act and behave when mistakes happen, either to us or because of us.

Every one of us makes mistakes; sometimes even big ones. The issue is not whether we make mistakes. It's how we handle the mistakes we make, and how we handle the mistakes of others; because how we react to imperfection is the key to defining our own perfection.

In the Book of Proverbs, King Solomon writes, "A righteous man falls seven times and rises. An evil man falls but once." This means if you are a good person who makes mistakes, you will always rise again no matter how low you fall. There are many stumbling blocks along the way and we are bound to stumble, and stumble again. However, it is crucial that we see our mistakes as mere setbacks, and not as defining moments. We must not identify either ourselves or others solely based on those mistakes. This is not what we are about. Rather, we need to move beyond our past mistakes and hopefully strive towards our own level of perfection.

We should never see ourselves as being incapable of moving past what we have done. Like the baseball pitcher, perfection is our goal. We would all like to be perfect. However, we're not, and sometimes, like with Armando Galarraga, through no fault of our own. No matter how many mistakes we make, and no matter how often others have hurt us, we must always strive to achieve our own level of perfection.

When we stumble or fail, and we are all bound to do so, let us own up to our mistakes. When others hurt us, let us be forgiving of them, and then let us continue to exhibit these traits every day of our lives. Remember, how we react to imperfection is the key to defining our own perfection. It is how we reach our level of God's perfection, and how we act most Godlike; by forgiving others as we ask God to forgive us.

Israel's Values　9

There isn't a time it seems, when one doesn't pick up a newspaper, watch television, or see online, a distorted view of the State of Israel. Without getting into all the policy debates, pros and cons of the peace process, or any similar issue, it behooves us to take a step back and realize that Israel, despite its faults, and face it, no country is perfect, behaves in a way which no other civilized country behaves.

I would be remiss in this book if I didn't at least point out two of many instances which demonstrate true Jewish and Israeli values, and how, whether the rest of the world cares to admit it or not, the State of Israel, and its citizens, have shown us how to be an "Or Lagoyim," a light unto the nations.

The first is how we value our own. We've all seen the images from Israel over the years of coffins containing the remains of dead soldiers being transferred across the border one way, while convicted terrorists are released and walk freely across the border the other way. And yet Israel continues to exchange convicted terrorists for the bodies of dead soldiers.

While the entire nation rejoiced in the fact that Gilad Schalit was finally released alive after over five years in a Hamas prison, think of the cost. Over one thousand terrorists freed to murder again. As articulated by Rabbi Daniel Gordis, we showed the world that each and every Jewish life is important and that we value life above all else.

The rest of the world might not share our values. No other country would do what we do, exchanging murderers for one young soldier, or even for the remains of our own. No matter what the risks or repercussions, we maintain our values in even the most difficult, painful and trying of circumstances.

We don't only preserve and protect our own lives. The second incident shows how we also do our utmost to preserve and protect the lives of our enemies, of killers of our children. This is because of another value we hold dear; "You shall love the stranger, for you were strangers in the land of Egypt." Again, despite what we read about in the newspapers or see on television, this commandment is still observed, in a way that Moses probably would never have dreamed of in his wildest imagination.

A few year ago a Jerusalem police officer named Shuki Sofer was murdered by terrorists. It was an incident which received little or no media attention in the US. It turned out that one of the terrorists had a six year old daughter who needed surgery to remove a tumor in her eye.

Where do you think she went to get the tumor removed? Jerusalem's Hadassah Ein Kerem Hospital, that's where.

Who paid for this hospitalization and procedure you might ask? An Israeli non-profit organization, that's who!

Imagine what would have happened if the Israeli security authorities had refused to allow the girl an entry permit to Jerusalem. So called human rights organizations would have immediately raised a stink about another example of those terrible Israelis mistreating a poor Arab girl. Can you see the story and the images? A sick Palestinian girl, concerned parents, and a military roadblock preventing her from receiving needed medical treatment.

Instead, those awful Israelis showed compassion to the family. Without even getting the Supreme Court or human rights organizations involved, the girl was treated at the Jerusalem hospital without question. Why? Because "You shall love the stranger, for you were strangers in the land of Egypt;" because we value saving a life above all else.

Despite Israeli doctors saving his daughter's life, her father the terrorist could not get rid of his hatred. According to the timeline constructed during the investigation, the terrorist said that he stayed by his daughter's bed at the hospital and he continued to plan the murder he later carried out at the very same time his daughter was in the hospital. This is what the terrorist was preoccupied with while Jewish medical teams treated his daughter as if she was their own. And the world continues to ask why we have roadblocks!

Why do we show such compassion to our enemies when all we do is get hate and terror in return? Let me offer you another reason to love the stranger; a reason which goes all the way back to when God first promised the land to Abraham.

God singled out a chosen people and a Promised Land for specific universal purposes. Abraham and his descendants, right on down to us, were charged to create a society based on principles of justice and righteousness. This society was to serve as a light unto the nations, an "Or Lagoyim," as this ideal later became known.

God made this promise to Abraham immediately following the destruction of Sodom and Gomorrah, because those cities represented the exact opposite of what Judaism represented. As the Torah states, "For I have singled him out, that he may instruct his children and his posterity to keep the way of the Lord by doing what is just and right, in order that the Lord may bring about for Abraham what He has promised him." This verse, from Genesis, might just be the crux of our entire value system.

God's promise to Abraham is conditional. Only, if his descendants build and maintain a society that is right and just, the exact opposite of Sodom and Gomorrah, will they not only inherit the Land of Canaan forever, but will also become a blessing for the world. Because we continue to maintain the ideal of loving the stranger, we also continue to merit the land of Israel.

It is this ideal which has sustained us throughout the centuries. It is our concern for the welfare of the stranger, that defines who we are and what we value. Justice and righteousness are to be measured by our treatment of the other, of the stranger, even if he is a terrorist. This is why we are now in possession of the Land of Israel.

We learn that if we want to maintain that possession, not only now, but forever, we must continue to love the stranger, as painful as that is, and as abhorrent as that is. In the end, we can hold our heads high, no matter the world's condemnation.

Finally, there's a corollary to the commandment to love the stranger. If we love the stranger so much, if we can treat the sick child of a terrorist and not ask for anything in return, shouldn't we love and treat our fellow Jews the same way? If we don't, that's a sure fire way of losing our inheritance to the land that God has promised us.

We must always keep in mind God's promise to Abraham and behave accordingly. We are worthy of the Land of Israel not because of might, but because of right. And that's "right," not in terms of a civil right, but "right" in terms of how we behave; that we behave righteously. Not only towards the stranger, although that's obviously important, but also how we behave towards our fellow Jews.

PART V
COMMUNITY AND CIVILITY

THE BEST OF TIMES; THE WORST OF TIMES 1

If we were to quote Charles Dickens, "It was the best of times; it was the worst of times," the generation of the desert could certainly be described as the best of times. All the people's needs were taken care of. They had no responsibilities to earn a living; no land to care for. All they had to do was eat manna and prepare to enter the Land of Canaan! On the other hand, it was also the worst of times because the majority of the fourth Book of the Torah, Numbers, aka "Kvetching in the Desert," relates the complaints and problems the Israelites dealt with over their forty years of wandering in the desert; from revolts over Moses and Aaron's leadership, to the episode of the spies, and concluding with Moses striking the rock.

The generation that experienced Egyptian slavery, was redeemed from Egypt, witnessed the miracle of the parting of the Red Sea, and received the Torah at Mount Sinai, was also the very same generation which complained, and revolted, and which ultimately failed in its mission to conquer the Promised Land, and died in the wilderness. That generation had it all and seen it all. Yet it constantly wanted more. It was never satisfied.

We are living in a similar era. In many ways things couldn't be better for the Jewish people, especially in America. For example, there are currently three Jewish Justices on the Supreme Court. For a group which represents approximately one and one half per cent of the population, having Jews comprise one third of our nation's highest Court is something to be proud of!

When the most recent Jewish Justice, Elana Kagan, was appointed in 2010, there were numerous references to Kagan's Jewish background in the media. Nevertheless, it was never an issue. Yes, the story of her bat mitzvah was interesting, and her remark about eating Chinese food on Christmas was funny. However, in reading various accounts of the nomination, from many sources and across the political spectrum, the criticism, if any, had nothing to do with her being Jewish, but rather with other issues, like ideology and qualifications.

In contrast, when Louis Brandeis was appointed as the first Jewish Justice in 1916, the anti-Semitic outcry was enormous. One sitting Justice refused to speak to him and wouldn't even pose for the annual picture if Brandeis was in it. Today, nearly one hundred years later, we can have three Jewish Justices and no one thinks twice. Not only that, but over eight per cent of the 2010 Congress identified themselves as Jews, including thirteen Senators.

Heady times! The best of times! But like in the desert, with the best of times comes the worst of times too.

In 2010, Brandeis University, a school named after Justice Louis Brandeis, with a large Jewish population, invited Israeli Ambassador Michael Oren to be its commencement speaker and to bestow upon him an honorary degree. Brandeis's student newspaper, criticized the choice, writing that "Mr. Oren is a divisive and inappropriate choice for keynote speaker at commencement, and we disapprove of the university's decision to grant someone of his polarity on this campus that honor." Ambassador Oren is a polarizing figure because, as the editorial continues, "The Israeli-Palestinian conflict is a hotly contested political issue, one that inspires students with serious positions on the topic to fervently defend and promote their views."

It's hard to imagine that a University named after the first Jewish Supreme Court Justice, a University with a large Jewish student body, would find it inappropriate to be addressed by the Israeli Ambassador. This incident shows that maybe things aren't so good for the Jews; that like the desert generation we also take things for granted, such as the existence of the State of Israel. In that regard we are like the desert generation. Our priorities are misplaced; we have our heads in the sand. We take things like Jewish Justices for granted, while at the same time we don't think twice about criticizing the appearance of the Israeli Ambassador.

After all, it's only Israel. It's no big deal. We're all Americans. Elena Kagan's religion means nothing. There's nothing special there. Nothing for us to be proud of. The rise in anti-Semitism brought on by the economic crisis, on blogs, all over the internet? It's blown out of proportion. It's just a tiny fringe minority. Everything's fine so long as we keep our heads in the sand.

Whether we are living in the best of times or we are living in the worst of times is therefore up to us. Do we want to take advantage of this possibly being the best of times and celebrate not only the continuing success of Jews in America but also our pride in, and success of Israel? If so, then we can make it the best of times. Or do we want to take it all for granted; stick our heads in the sand, and ignore the dangers around us? If that's the case, then it surely will be the worst of times.

It is truly up to us to be proud on the one hand but vigilant on the other and not to take what we have for granted; to not take the attitude that anti-Semitism is completely erased, or to take the attitude that Israel is only about oppression and apartheid. It is up to us to continue to make this the best of times because far too many have lived through the worst of times.

The way we can ensure this being the best of times is by taking a lesson from the Torah which was given to the desert generation; the same ones who kvetched and revolted and made what could have been the best of times into the worst of times. God commanded that every Jew be counted. Not only that, but that every head should be counted! We count every Jew because every Jew is important; because every Jew means something; because given our small numbers, which we seem to forget at times, we can't afford to lose any Jew, and we can't afford not to be united in pursuit of our common goals. We continually count our numbers to remind us what a small minority we are; to remind us of our need to be vigilant to protect our interests. We count to remind ourselves of the dangers if our numbers get too low.

Furthermore, we count the heads and not the feet, the hands, or the noses, because the head controls our body. It is the center of our intellect. It is a reminder that we must keep our heads out of the sand and realize what we must do to fight the anti-Semitism and Israel bashing that still exists. If our heads are in the sand we can't be counted. We can't respond. We can't speak up. So we must count the heads and then use our heads to truly make this the best of times, as it has such potential to be. The choice is ours.

After the editorial in the Brandeis newspaper was published, many Brandeis students voiced strong support for Ambassador Oren's appearance in newspapers, on blogs, and on Facebook pages. Perhaps most significantly, when fifteen students came to the University President's office to protest Ambassador Oren's selection, the President showed them a student initiated petition with over 4,000 signatures..... supporting Oren's selection. A suggestion was then floated in the University Senate to register official displeasure at Oren's invitation. It got nowhere.

This incident demonstrates that good things can happen to us and for us if only we keep our heads out of the sand and stand up and be counted. It shows us how we can transform the possible worst of times, into truly the best of times. It is up to us which path we take.

AHAVAT YISRAEL 2

The prophet Ezekiel often railed against the divisions between the Jewish people, as represented by the northern kingdom of Israel and the southern kingdom of Judah. If you think those divisions have healed some twenty five hundred years after Ezekiel's prophesy, think again! Just look at the divisions in the Jewish community today, and not just the political divisions in Israel. Look at the disputes and fights between different branches, sects, and denominations of Judaism, with some claiming to have a monopoly on defining Judaism, it's rules, its practices and its members, as well as the vitriolic responses of average, ordinary Jews in defending their own view of Judaism and in criticizing and lambasting fellow Jews who don't agree with those views.

Let me share with you three events which illustrate these divisions, each of which is horrifying and problematic on its own. Taken together though, we see why this is so problematic for the Jewish community.

The first story concerns Women of the Wall. A few years ago an Israeli woman, a medical student, was arrested while praying at the Western Wall, because she and her fellow female Jews were wearing tallitot and were reading from their own Torah which they had brought. It's one thing to have a mechitzah at the Wall. It's another thing to separate men and women. It might even be ok to prevent women from reading the Torah or wearing a tallit since it might be offensive to some. I don't agree. I think it's wrong. However, at least there's a valid argument why that would be so. But to arrest someone for wearing a tallit? To arrest a fellow Jew because she had a Torah? That is going way too far. That stretches the bounds of ahavat Yisrael - love of one's fellow Jew. And it is the embodiment of sinat chinam, baseless hatred among fellow Jews.

The second story took place in Madrid, Spain where a thirteen year old boy was prohibited from being buried in a Jewish cemetery because the Beit Din that officiated over the boy's conversion was made up of Masorti, non-Orthodox rabbis. He was buried outside the main cemetery in an area in the very lower corner separated from the larger site. Whatever one's opinion or position on the appropriate conversion standards, what is most telling about this story is the flurry of vicious comments it elicited on the Jerusalem Post website where the story was published. We don't need to look for posts by anti-Semites commenting on Jewish related stories. We have our own people, fellow Jews, doing it for us, calling each other names, blasting each other's brand of Judaism, or the way it's practiced. That's sinat chinam. Baseless hatred.

Then we have the continuing shameful attempt by the extremists in the Haredi or ultra-orthodox community to impose their standards on the rest of Israeli society, including not only the secular, but even those who are Orthodox or Haredi themselves but who don't follow the same Haredi outlook. We have witnessed attacks on Israeli soldiers in the West Bank, the trashing of a book store for selling secular books (which of course promotes promiscuity), vandalism against an ice cream shop, because eating ice cream in public is a sexual act and also promotes promiscuity, forcing women to sit in the back of public bus, and not permitting women soldiers to sing at military functions.

Most recently, in the orthodox community of Beit Shemesh, an eight year old girl, the Orthodox daughter of Americans who made aliyah, was spit on and called a whore because she was dressed immodestly in their opinion. An eight year old Jewish girl was afraid to walk to her Jewish school because she was harassed and threatened by other Jews who didn't see her as being "Jewish enough." She was harassed by Jews who feel that they have a monopoly on deciding how everyone else should behave.

Fortunately, the response by Israelis to that eight year old girl's story was overwhelming. Haaretz reported that it had received calls from "mainstream" Haredi who denounced these incidents and wanted to let the public know that they were being done by a small minority of extremists. A rally was held in Beit Shemesh, attended by thousands across the Israeli spectrum. Young and old. Secular and religious. Orthodox and Masorti. Members of the Knesset. They all came to denounce what has been happening. To protest religious violence and fanaticism.

As Jews, no matter our own practices or beliefs, we must all love our fellow Jew, no matter theirs. This is the essence of Kiddush Hashem, honoring and sanctifying God. We don't do ourselves any favors in the eyes of the world when we engage in this sort of behavior, because insulting or attacking other Jews is never the way God fearing, Torah observant Jews, should behave. Being accepting of all Jews, no matter our differences, and bringing them closer to God and Torah through loving kindness, not through violence, is the way that a true God fearing, Torah observant Jew, should behave.

This is why Ezekiel's message must resonate loudly to us today. Ezekiel took two sticks, he wrote Ephraim on one and Judah on the other. He joined them together so they became one stick. And he repeated this message from God.

"I am going to take the stick of Joseph, which is in the hand of Ephraim, and all the tribes of Ephraim associated with him, and I will place the stick of Judah upon it and make them into one stick...I will make them one nation ...never again shall they be divided... I will cleanse them. Then they shall be My people and I will be their God."

We must therefore resolve to work together to engage in "Ahavat Yisrael," the love of our fellow Jews, to end the "sinat chinam," the baseless hatred that exists among us, and to fulfill Ezekiel's prophecy of becoming one united people.

WHO DECIDES? 3

Who is a Jew? While that question has been the subject of some controversy and debate over the years, what has not been the subject of debate is that it is the Jewish religious authorities who usually get to decide that question. In other words, we, the Jewish community, are the arbiters of resolving our own internal membership issues; not any outside entity. That all changed a few years back when Britain's Supreme Court issued a ruling in late 2009 whose impact is potentially quite far-reaching and which unfortunately has not received much attention here in America, especially in the Jewish media. Briefly stated, the court held that defining one's membership in the Jewish faith on parentage alone is "racist and discriminatory."

Now in all fairness, Britain has no written constitution, no constitutional separation of church and state, and apparently no abstention doctrine whereby the courts won't get involved in deciding religious doctrinal matters. It also directly funds parochial schools. Thus, the likelihood of a similar case and·

195

a similar decision occurring in the United States is relatively small. Nevertheless, this case bears commenting on because of its implications for the Jewish community.

The case involved the Jewish Free School, a government funded Jewish school in London, which under British law, as a "faith school," is allowed to give preference to members of the Jewish religion in admissions, although it is barred from discriminating on racial grounds.

A student applied for admission to this school but was turned down because his mother wasn't born Jewish. The child and the mother were converted to Judaism by a Progressive rabbi, a conversion which was not recognized by Britain's Orthodox establishment. Britain's chief rabbi therefore ruled that the child was not Jewish and not eligible for admission to the JFS. The child's parents sued the school claiming racial discrimination.

Whether this child's conversion was valid or not is not the issue. The issue here is that the secular, non-Jewish courts decided the question of "Who is a Jew?" And they decided that basing one's membership in the Jewish faith on lineage and parentage is discriminatory and racist. In other words, the Supreme Court effectively said that Judaism's way of defining its own membership, as we've done for over 3,500 years, is illegal!

The Court's decision thus requires Jewish schools to rely on the belief and practice of a child to determine if that child is Jewish and eligible for admission to a Jewish school. Synagogue attendance, observing holidays, and participating in Jewish rituals will now be the deciding factors in determining if one is Jewish or not. Why belief and practice? Because those are the criteria for determining religion in the Christian world. And now, in England, those are the criteria in the Jewish world as well.

As Lord Brown noted, essentially we must now apply a "Non-Jewish definition of who is Jewish." Thus, immersed in a culture in which "religion" is defined by issues of belief and practice, these justices were in a sense bewildered by Jewish religious law that insists that to be Jewish, one must be a member of the Jewish people, either by birth, meaning that one's mother was Jewish, or by choice, meaning conversion.

The truly ironic part of this decision is that Hitler didn't care if a Jew practiced Judaism or not, was observant or not, or was converted by the Orthodox or Progressive or Conservative or Reform. To Hitler if you had Jewish blood, if an ancestor was Jewish, then you were Jewish. At least Hitler understood the importance of parentage to Judaism.

While many might be overjoyed that the Court struck down an Orthodox-only standard of conversion, bear in mind that this decision also essentially struck down a Reform standard of patrilineal descent and any other standard of lineal descent as well. It struck down the very way in which all mainstream branches of Judaism define who is a Jew, define citizenship. This is a serious problem for the Jewish community, all Jewish communities, who are at great pains to maintain our own rules while respecting the law of the land.

When the secular authorities determine "Who is a Jew," when the courts choose sides in an inter-denominational debate on the validity of conversions, on how we define our own membership criteria, or on any other standard of religious practice, there can be no good result. Unless we, the Jewish community, begin to address these issues in a respectful dialogue among ourselves, we run the risk that others, specifically non-Jews, who certainly don't have the best interests of the Jewish community at heart, will make these decisions for us. That is something which we cannot afford to let happen.

CHRISTMAS 4

As Jews, it is fair to say that we are quite comfortable in American society. This is because of the freedoms given to us here, especially the freedom of religion. However, despite these freedoms and our comfortable status, the Christmas season is our most blatant reminder that we are in fact a religious minority in America.

Christmas is a Christian religious holiday; period! There is no reason to deny it or hide from it, and it doesn't make us any less Jewish or any less American by acknowledging this fact. Nor does it do us any good by trying to make Christmas into a secular American holiday. Secularizing Christmas as a way of justifying its status as a national holiday we can all celebrate, demeans both the religious nature of the holiday and the Christian faith itself. As religious people ourselves, we should not go along with that.

Christmas is and should be a religious holiday which happens to be observed by approximately ninety per cent of our fellow American citizens. If they observe this as a holiday, then it makes sense that it be considered a national holiday as well. It makes sense that government offices are closed on Christmas just as public schools are closed on Rosh Hashanah and Yom Kippur in areas where there is a large Jewish population.

Furthermore, the idea that it is politically incorrect to wish someone a Merry Christmas is also wrong. Merry Christmas is a Christian's way of celebrating their holiday. There is no need to be offended by that just because we don't celebrate this holiday. We should respect those of other faiths, and their demonstration of that faith, especially those who take their faith seriously.

As Jews, our response to Christmas cannot be so negative, because with Christmas all around us, it's both unreasonable and unrealistic to say that we have to ignore it. We can enjoy the holiday music, for example; not necessarily the purely religious hymns, but the seasonal songs like White Christmas, which was written by a Jew, Irving Berlin. We can appreciate and acknowledge the beauty of Christmas; the trees, the ornaments, the decorations, the lights, the music, as well as it's religious and cultural importance to our Christian friends and neighbors, while at the same time always remembering that it is not our celebration. It is not our holiday.

If we are strong and secure in our own Jewish commitment, there really is little danger that appreciating another's holiday will somehow permanently threaten our own Jewish identity. At the same time, we do well to remember that appreciating Christmas should not give us an excuse to make it our own, because that will only lead to confusion, assimilation, and ultimately, the loss of our Jewish identity.

Another way for us to relate to Christmas is to understand that many of the Christmas themed movies, such as "It's a Wonderful Life" or "Miracle on 34th Street," contain themes which are very much in keeping with Jewish thinking. We can watch and enjoy these Christmas movies because the messages they contain are universal, human interest stories, not only for Christians, not only for that time of year, but for all people, all the time.

"It's a Wonderful Life" is the story of a man who thinks his life isn't worth living until an angel shows him what other people's lives would be like if he hadn't lived. Now substitute Moses for Jimmy Stewart. What if Moses, fed up with the way the Israelites treated him, decided it was better that he had never lived. Where would we be without Moses? What would have happened if he had never lived? Might we still be slaves in Egypt?

When George, the character played by Jimmy Stewart, despairs over his life, when he feels that the bad outweighs the good, we can give him a little bit of Jewish advice and say to him that on Rosh Hashanah we ask that our good deeds outweigh the bad, and let God be the merciful judge. Finally, at the end of the film, when George comes to realize how many lives he has touched and how much of an impact he has had on so many others, he can at last acknowledge the truth of his brother's toast that he is "The richest man in town." Or to quote Pirkei Avot, "Who is rich? One who is satisfied with his portion." It's A Wonderful Jewish Life, isn't it?

While we don't believe in Santa Claus, "Miracle on 34th Street" still resonates in our Jewish souls. After all, Jews do believe in miracles. The Exodus, the crossing of the Red

Sea, the State of Israel are all miracles for us. It is why we say every day in our liturgy, "Vayaaminu badonai u'vMoshe avdo?" We believe in God and in His servant Moses! It might not exactly be Santa Claus, but we do believe in something powerful and supernatural. It is that belief and faith which sustains us. It is far better to have that kind of belief, even if it's about something that is not objectively provable, than to have no faith or belief at all. We are all better off believing in God, in His ability to care for us, create miracles for us, and bring us joy in life, rather than not believing in Him at all, or believing that God is some kind of fairy tale or mythical figure.

We should therefore treat Christmas in two distinct ways. First, we must affirm the messages contained in movies such as "It's A Wonderful Life" and "Miracle on 34th Street" because we can relate those themes to our own heritage and values. At the same time we also need to remember that the religious message of Christmas, one which we do not believe in, is about celebrating a lifestyle and theology which is not ours. If we secularize Christmas, if we say that it's okay for us to "celebrate" Christmas because it's all about the season or feel good movies, then we will eventually come to forget that there are messages which we don't believe in which still pervade the holiday. We are hurting ourselves if we forget that fact.

At Christmastime, as Jewish-Americans, let us be thankful for the freedoms we have here, let us be open to celebrating the holiday with our non-Jewish friends and neighbors, and most importantly, let us remember that the more religion there is in Christmas, the more aware we hopefully become of our own religious traditions. Although we can admire and respect the ecumenical, universal messages of peace on Earth and goodwill to man, let us never forget that Christmas is not our holiday, it is not our theological message, and that appreciation does not mean appropriation or even imitation.

INAUGURATION 5

The Ten Commandments tells us not to worship idols or make graven images. This has led to the centuries old prohibition of Jews going into a Church. For many, this prohibition still applies today, in twenty-first century America, where we live side by side with our non-Jewish neighbors, and are often asked and invited to share with them in their religious traditions and celebrations. In light of this reality, should we still be prohibited from going into a Church or a Mosque, and if so, might there be exceptions?

I have read that there are two models of leadership and behavior in modern Jewish life. One model relies on, and follows, almost exclusively, the sacred texts of our tradition, for clear direction; while the other model, looks at those same texts for guidance, but tempers that guidance with a realistic understanding of the issues confronting modern Jewish life. The model one chooses says a great deal about us individually as Jews, as well as how we view modern Jewry and the world in which we live.

If we go by the second model of behavior and leadership; if we allow ourselves to look beyond the obvious text to see the bigger picture, especially as it relates to world events, then maybe we will come away with a clearer view of what the Torah is really telling us.

As the Israelites were gathered at Mount Sinai, before receiving the Torah, God told them the following, "You shall be my treasured possession among all the peoples....you shall be to me a kingdom of priests and a holy nation." This is who we are and who we're supposed to be. We are supposed to be holy. We are supposed to be an "Or Lagoyim," a light unto the nations.

How do we accomplish this?

One way is by putting aside some of our own personal agendas or attachment to text, to do what is best for the Jewish community. Let me demonstrate by telling you a tale of two Churches. Here's the first tale.

It's the story of a convert to Judaism who was originally raised Catholic. When her closest friend was getting married in a big Church wedding, she told her friend that she couldn't attend, because her rabbi informed her that as a Jew she wasn't permitted to go into a Church.

Naturally, her friend didn't understand. What was the big deal about going to Church for a once in a lifetime celebration? She e-mailed her friend, apologizing profusely for causing her pain. She told her friend how much she loved her and detailed how much that friend meant to her. She left messages with her friend's mother and father, who fondly remembered feeding her. Eventually, she stopped bothering them. That once close friend never called again; never wrote again. She never heard from her again.

Here's the second tale.

On the day following the inauguration of President Obama a prayer service was held at the National Cathedral in Washington, D.C. Representatives of many religions were invited to participate, including, of course Judaism. Judaism wasn't represented by just one rabbi. There was a representative from the Conservative movement, a representative from the Reform movement, and yes, even an Orthodox rabbi, Rabbi Haskel Lookstein, of Kehilath Jeshurun in New York.

Rabbi Lookstein's participation was controversial. The Rabbinical Council of America, the umbrella organization of the Orthodox rabbinate, criticized Rabbi Lookstein's participation on the ground that "Under any circumstances, it was against halacha to go into a church." In the face of this criticism and threat of disciplinary action, Rabbi Lookstein took a courageous stand. He attended the service as the representative of the Orthodox community. He was willing to face the threat of discipline from the RCA because he felt that his participation would not only be an act of patriotism on his part, but that he would be rendering a very important service to the Orthodox Jewish community. "Imagine," he said, "that, in front of the new President and his new administration, a Reform Rabbi and a Conservative Rabbi participated in that service and there was no Orthodox representative. How would that look?"

Which of those two stories really reflects on what it means to be a kingdom of priests and a holy nation today?

Forget the specifics and intricacies of Halacha. Rather, think about what it means to engage in Kiddush Hashem - to be part of a kingdom of priests and a holy nation. Think about what it means to be a light unto the nations.

The example set by Rabbi Lookstein, an Orthodox rabbi, reminds us that we do not live in a small, isolated shtetl anymore. We now live in the real world. We live in a country where we are part and parcel of the fabric of its society. We live in a country where we have attained the highest positions of power in business, industry and government. We live in a country where our religious leaders are invited to meet and pray with the President of the United States.

We can go to Church without praying in a way which violates the tenets of our faith. And we can go into a church without bowing, kneeling, or taking any other action which our religion frowns upon. I believe that we are strong and knowledgeable enough to do so. But avoiding the Church altogether, sends the wrong message; a message Rabbi Lookstein, for one, understood.

We must always draw our strength and our values from our Torah and from our tradition. We must begin with the words of the Ten Commandments, for it is the Ten Commandments which first gave us those words "Thou Shall" and "Thou Shalt Not." But our beliefs, our actions, and our behavior, in today's world, are vastly different than that envisioned and codified by our ancestors many centuries ago. This is why to live by the principles of Kiddush Hashem, the sanctification of God's name, and to truly be a kingdom of priests and a holy nation, we must figure out a way to still say "Yes" without sacrificing our core values.

It's very easy to say "No." But the real strength of Judaism is finding a way to say "yes" in situations like these. We must be able to say "Yes We Can" in order to continue to live our lives fully as Jews, in the twenty-first century, in an ever changing, multi-cultural world.

A Visit To Church 6

W hen Temple Beth Kodesh celebrated its 36th Anniversary, the newly appointed Mayor of Boynton Beach, Florida, Woodrow Hay, attended our services. I met Mayor Hay and his wife in the lobby and I invited him to sit on the bimah along with the vice-Mayor. Mayor Hay is not Jewish. His response to my invitation? "Would that be ok? Am I allowed to sit there?" I said of course, and that we were honored by his presence.

During the course of the service I learned that Mayor Hay is a Baptist, serves as a lay minister in his Church, and would soon be ordained. Mayor Hay participated in our services, tried to follow along, and enjoyed what we were doing. He not only congratulated us on our milestone, but also spoke about how he was moved by our services, and thought that in a few more visits he could really get the hang of it. More importantly, he invited us to attend his Church, to also see how they worship.

So what happened? A number of us, being impressed with his sincerity, and his respect for us, agreed to reciprocate and attend his services at the St John Missionary Baptist Church. We went because we were invited. We went because we wanted to see and learn about another faith. Most of all we went to show respect to those who showed us respect.

We were shown warmth and hospitality by everyone in the Church. We were warmly greeted. We were asked to sit in the front pews. Mayor Hay, who was leading the service in the absence of their senior minister who was ill, insisted that I sit with him on the pulpit. Later on in the service, he invited me to address his congregation. I cherished the opportunity to do so. It was an honor for me, but more importantly, it was an honor for all of us who attended, and for all who are part of the Jewish community.

I was grateful for the opportunity because by attending, by participating, by speaking, we had the opportunity to show that Jews are not parochial, living separate from the rest of the community. We had the opportunity to show what Jews are really like and how respectful we are of other faiths. By doing so, by being visible in our communities as representatives of Judaism, we had the opportunity, just by our mere presence, to hopefully play a small part in possibly combating any anti-Semitic stereotypes others may have of Jews. Additionally, let's not forget of course the support Israel receives from the Christian community. It's a way of saying thank you and fostering continued support.

We came away from the experience moved by the joy and devotion we witnessed. We learned about their faith and their mode of worship. We saw that there is a lot more that we have in common in terms of how we address God than the theological differences which divide us. For example, we heard the term "Praise the Lord." We heard that over and over and it sounded foreign to us. It really shouldn't have because we say the same thing. Only we say it in Hebrew. We say "Baruch Hashem." It means "Praise the Lord."

I can attend a Church service because I am secure enough in my own Judaism that I am not afraid of losing any of my faith or my beliefs. I can attend a Church service because I am secure enough in my own Judaism that I can be open to learning about other faiths, be open to learning how other faiths conduct their services, and be open to learning how other faiths inspire their congregants. Isn't that what religion is all about? Inspiring others to serve God? As the famous Jewish composer Craig Taubman wrote, "All the talk about interfaith dialogue is just that - talk. We sit around and talk. Better to go and watch and participate and learn and invite."

We are charged to be a goy kadosh, a holy nation. What better way of being holy than by showing our non-Jewish neighbors that we care, and that we treat them with the same respect and courtesy as they treat us? We can be respectful of other faiths and participate with them without having to violate the core tenets and principles of our own religion.

Although Mayor Hay was invited to sit on the bimah, of course we couldn't offer him an aliyah. In his Church, I was asked to lead a responsive reading..... from the Gospel of Luke. I respectfully declined. Mayor Hay immediately understood why I had to do so. That is mutual respect born out of a willingness to share and participate, but never be forced or required to do something that violates one's own religion or conscience.

Jews, Catholics, Baptists, Hindus, Moslems. The list goes on. We have many differences. But we must respect each other's beliefs even if we disagree. And we can disagree, even theologically, even strenuously, without having to demonize them or anyone else for not believing and practicing the same way we do. Similarly, we ask the same respect from those who disagree with us. Feel free to disagree, feel free to believe what you want, but please respect our religion, our beliefs, and allow us to practice and observe it as we see fit, without any limitation, restriction or derision. That is what makes America great. That is something that we, as a minority religion, must celebrate, and hold sacred.

We must always engage in Kiddush Hashem, the sanctification of God's name. We are part of a goy kadosh, a holy nation. We are to be an or lagoyim, a light unto the nations. The way to do all of that, the way to live like that, is to show warmth, hospitality, kindness and respect to others, to put aside some pre-conceived notions, and to do what is best for the Jewish community. As I wrote in the previous chapter, and it bears repeating here, it behooves us to realize that our status in today's world is very different than that envisioned and codified by our ancestors many centuries ago. That is because we live in a country where we are part and parcel of the fabric of its society, and where our religious leaders are invited to meet and pray with both the President of the United States and the Mayor of Boynton Beach, Florida.

We should therefore look at this experience as the honor it truly was, and use this experience to create similar experiences, similar bonds, with our neighbors, to show them what Jews are really about. This is how we engage in Kiddush Hashem, how we sanctify God's name. We do so whenever and wherever we stand up, whether in shul, or in Church, and we say that we are God's people.

MAKE ME A SANCTUARY 7

D espite the fact that we are presented with a myriad of details concerning God's command to Moses to build a sanctuary, there is only one reason given for God's command; "Make Me a sanctuary that I may dwell among them." God wanted Moses to build Him a home here on earth. Notice though that God didn't say, in order "That I may dwell in it;" rather, God says, the purpose is "That I may dwell *among them*." Among whom? Among us; among the people; among His people. God wanted us to look at the sanctuary as a reminder that He is here among us. That sanctuary can be the Holy Temple, it can be a synagogue, and it can be anyplace we believe is a suitable location for God to dwell among us. It can even be a piece of land.

This piece of land to which I'm referring is not the Land of Israel, but the United States of America. The United States has been a sanctuary, a safe haven, for persecuted people from all over the world since its founding, especially for Jews. This is why we believe that God dwells here too, in America, among us, and not just in Jerusalem. It is why we can share our Jewish values with our fellow citizens. On the other hand, if we want to believe this, if we want to see America as this sanctuary, we also have to accept American values as well, one of which is freedom of speech.

In January 2010, Michael Oren, the Israeli Ambassador to the United States, was invited to speak at the University of California at Irvine. A group of students, apparently all members of the Muslim Students Union, tried to stop the speech. The students came up with the following plan. They had been told that if they interrupted the speech, they would be arrested for disturbing a public event, so the students went sequentially, each interrupting the Ambassador once. Each student would stand up in the middle of the speech and start screaming out condemnation, which would trigger the wild applause of many other students in the audience. The student would then walk to the aisle to be arrested and escorted out by campus police.

As much as this incident may bother us, we must recognize that this is America and in America we have a right called Freedom of Speech. Dealing with speech we don't like, as uncivil as that speech may be, is part of being an American. It's the downside of our freedoms. However, that right to free speech is meaningless if anyone can show up to any event, and literally drown out a speech.

We have every right to hold a similar event, or make as many other speeches as we want, to try to counter a message we don't like. But we must respect another's right to speak, and the right of the audience to hear what he has to say. What those UC Irvine students did showed contempt for the underlying principles represented by our First Amendment. The free exchange of ideas is fundamental to democracy, and ultimately that is what these protestors attacked. We should also remember that the University is a sanctuary as well and that God is there too.

The best response to this incident came from Michael Oren himself. After the fourth disruption Oren took a twenty minute break. When he returned he said the following: "I've spent most of my life living in and studying the Middle East and one of the great and eternal cultural facets of the Middle East is hospitality...even if you do not agree with them, even if they're ostensibly your enemy... I'm your guest here and I'm asking for the Middle Eastern hospitality for your guest, I've come into your house." Yes, he's come to our house, our sanctuary, a space that we feel should be filled with God's presence, but unfortunately wasn't. This is why it behooves us to remember that this too is God's sanctuary and all must be made to feel welcome.

Around the same time as the UC Irvine incident, the New York Times Magazine carried a lengthy article entitled "How Christian Were The Founders?" The article detailed the efforts of the Texas School Board to include more references in their Social Studies curriculum to America being a Christian nation which was founded by Christians on Christian principles. For example, one Board member stated, "Many of the points that have been incorporated into the guidelines or that have been advanced by board members and their expert advisers ... thus instills the idea that America was founded as a project for the spread of Christianity." While I certainly don't qualify as an expert on this subject, my research would enable me to go on for pages with specific details and examples of why that quote is not entirely accurate.

Briefly, here's my take on the notion that America was founded as a "Christian Nation" or on Christian principles. Yes, America was founded by men who were mostly Christian, and yes, for many their Christian faith played a large role in their fight for American independence and freedom. However, these men also had widely differing views and opinions on what that Christianity meant. This included the view that their religious beliefs should not be incorporated into the institutions of the new government. Since many of our founders came to America to escape religious persecution, they were intent on granting religious liberty to all, not dictating to anyone what he or she should or shouldn't believe, and most importantly, not establishing a national religion or any one particular theological viewpoint.

If America was indeed founded as a Christian nation, then America is not, and cannot be, a sanctuary for all. And if it isn't a sanctuary for all, then God certainly doesn't reside here, among us. On the other hand, if God does reside here, then the opposite is true. America is a sanctuary, for all people, from all different nationalities, faiths and beliefs, and those differences must be respected.

There is a role for religion, for faith, and for values, in our public life. However, that role cannot come about through a distortion of our history, a distortion of the intentions of our founders, and disrespect for those who don't share the same views. The Muslim students didn't have the right to stop the Israeli Ambassador from speaking, and the Texas School Board doesn't have the right to impose their view that God only dwells in their sanctuary, and only among some people; only among those who share their views.

Incivility, claiming exclusive rights to God, is not making a sanctuary for God to dwell among us. Rather, let us strive to build true sanctuaries. Let us make our institutions true sanctuaries. Let us build safe havens, where civility, respect, and principles of love your neighbor are taught. Most importantly, let us build and maintain sanctuaries where differences are respected, as long as they are for the sake of heaven, and where everyone, despite these differences, has a place in this sanctuary.

If America is truly God's sanctuary, if our founders and if many of us today believe in God, and believe that this land is truly under God's providence, then it must be for all, and not just a select few. We built a country for God to be proud of, to dwell among us; but in so doing we must remember that the greatness and beauty of America is that it is everybody's God and everybody's sanctuary. This is what makes God "Shed His Grace On Thee!" It is why we say "God Bless America."

A DECADE AFTER 9/11 8

In response to a question posed by one of his professors, "Did God create everything that exists?" a young Albert Einstein bravely replied, "Yes he did!" "God created everything." After a further back and forth, Einstein then made the following statement; "Evil does not exist, sir, or at least it does not exist unto itself. Evil is simply the absence of God. It is just like darkness and cold, a word that man has created to describe the absence of God. God did not create evil. Evil is the result of what happens when man does not have God's love present in his heart. It's like the cold that comes when there is no heat, or the darkness that comes when there is no light."

Now Albert Einstein was many things. He was certainly a genius. But, quite frankly, no one ever accused him of being a Biblical scholar, because if he was he would have known that evil does exist and that God created evil, just like he created suffering. To put it simply - without evil, we have no definition, no knowledge, of what's good. Without suffering, there can be no compassion.

We know that God created evil from the Bible. In the very beginning, in the Garden of Eden, he created a tree of knowledge of good and evil. God spoke of people doing evil, like the generation of the flood, and the cities of Sodom and Gomorrah. God even said that people have a choice - to do good or do evil - to receive a blessing or a curse. So evil is not just the absence of God or of good. It is a standalone object of God's creation that exists so that we know what good is and how to behave that way.

A decade after 9/11, a day of ultimate evil, we still ask what lessons have we taken from that day; what has changed over the past ten years; and what are we doing about it? Judaism tells us that we must destroy evil. We have tried to do so but evil, the terrorists, those who seek to destroy not only Israel but America as well, are still here. Still thriving. Still plotting. In May 2011, U.S. Navy Seals killed Bin Laden. This didn't end Al Queda; it didn't end terrorism; and it didn't end evil.

Contrary to what Albert Einstein thinks, evil does exist. Just like the poor, just like suffering, evil will always exist. It's a part of God's master plan. It's part of God's creation. However, existing in order to teach us to appreciate the opposite - goodness, compassion, charity - is one thing. Thriving, allowing evil to thrive, is quite another.

This is why Judaism tells us that we bear responsibility for our actions. Those terrorists who attacked us, it is their fault, their responsibility. They are to blame. We don't blame the victims. We don't blame the world's political situation. We don't blame Israel or its policies. We don't blame American foreign policy. We don't blame intelligence failures. We place the blame squarely where it belongs; on those who planned, financed, aided and abetted, and carried out this evil. We must continue, all of us who care about good, to do so.

There's another way which Judaism teaches us how to respond to evil. If God did create evil, and if evil has a purpose, then what is it? Is there another way of overcoming it? The answer is yes which is why we should also take a moment and think of the good that came out of 9/11.

Recall the stories of heroism and bravery which we saw and read about. Recall how we were united as a people; how we were all New Yorkers, all Americans. Democrats and Republicans, Christian, Jew, Hindu, Buddhist and Moslem, everyone and anyone who believed in good, all united, all came together to help each other.

If there is one way to defeat evil, it is to combat evil with its opposite - goodness. If we continue to unite, continue to help each other, continue to do good for each other, continue to show that life goes on, then we have dealt those who seek to destroy our way of life a serious blow. However, if we neglect to do so, forgot how to do so, or do so only for a moment, and not for all times, and I'm sad to say we may have; then evil wins.

Theologically speaking, perhaps God allowed an act of unspeakable evil to occur in order to give us an opportunity to rise above it. So long as we continue to remember the evil, we must continue to take advantage of that opportunity; to continue to show that goodness conquers evil; to continue to show that those who perished did not die in vain.

We will never rid the world of all evil, but we have a duty to vanquish it when we can and when we are able. It is our commandment from the Torah. We can choose to be good or we can choose to be evil. We can choose to let goodness thrive or we can choose to let evil thrive. We can choose to ignore evil or we can choose to do something about it. We can choose to let our differences guide us, or we can choose to find what unites us. How we respond is our choice.

Finally, we conquer evil by not letting it conquer us. In June 2001, three months before 9/11, a suicide bomber murdered twenty one teenagers at The Dolphinarium nightclub in Tel Aviv, destroying the building in the process. A few days later, someone placed a sign on what used to be the front door. The sign contained three Hebrew words and simply read,

"Lo Nafsik Lirkod." We will not stop dancing!

These three words not only speak to who we are and what we stand for. They are a promise as well; a promise that we will always respond to evil. We will not let evil destroy us; we will not let evil stop us from living; and we will not let evil stop us from bonding together. Rather, if we can't totally eradicate evil, we then turn evil on its head and use it to show how we can come together to rebuild our lives and our communities.

Lo Nafsik Lirkod. We shall not stop dancing!

PART VI

LIFE-LONG LEARNING

Positive Judaism 1

My personal theology is what I like to call "Positive Judaism." Positive Judaism is the idea that instead of focusing on all the negatives in Judaism - the laws, the fasting, the overemphasis on past horrors - we change our focus to all the good and positive things there are about Judaism; our families, a Friday evening meal at home, Simchat Torah, Hanukkah, Purim, the Seder, Israel, and so much more.

Judaism cannot revolve solely around the High Holidays. They are but one part of the cycle of our Jewish existence. As I explained to a congregant who insisted that his inter-married son bring his children for High Holiday services in order to get them to love Judaism, "Why do you insist on boring them to death for four to five hours doing something they have no idea what they're doing or why they're doing it, and something which they only do once a year anyway? Instead, invite them for a Shabbat or Yom Tov dinner at home. Bring them to shul for Simchat Torah or Purim, where they'll spend one or two hours just having fun. That will be a better way to increase their Jewish identity. Increasing Jewish identity should be the goal for all of us, and it must begin as the primary goal of our Hebrew Schools.

If we raise our children with pride in being Jewish, understanding that it's good to be Jewish, then, as they get older and can absorb more, we can teach them more - the Hebrew language, Torah, texts, history, etc. Let's first teach them Jewish ethics and values, and that it's cool to be Jewish. Then, when they become adults, hopefully they will take advantage of the myriad of learning opportunities available to them, in actual courses and programs, as well as on the internet. Anyone, no matter their level of Judaic knowledge, can, and must, take advantage of these very same learning opportunities. Judaism is a life-long journey. It doesn't stop at one's bar or bat mitzvah. There is always more to learn, absorb, experience, and do. The opportunities for Jewish learning have never been greater.

Here's an example. I was once teaching a class on Shabbat from the Mishnah. I asked the class to make two columns and write down the positive aspects of Shabbat in Column A and the negative aspects of Shabbat in column B. Of course Column B won out, especially as the class was going through the text looking for examples. Then I asked them to focus on Column A and think of ways to make Shabbat more positive. The ideas started flowing.

I posed the following scenario to them. If you come to shul on a Friday night and have a relatively brief kabbalat Shabbat service; then go home to a Shabbat meal with kiddush and challah and zemirot, Shabbat songs, which you share with family and friends, then guess what? You've not only enjoyed

Shabbat, you've not only made it a positive experience, but in doing so, you didn't go out shopping, you didn't go to the movies, you didn't engage in any of the prohibited negative behaviors! Instead of focusing on the negative aspects, you were too busy doing, and hopefully enjoying, the positive, joyful things which Judaism is all about.

And..... if you happen to venture out to the movies after your Shabbat dinner, at least you've recognized, experienced, and brought a little bit of the joy of Judaism into your lives. Maybe, if you came away from that experience realizing that it wasn't so bad...... maybe, if you're willing to admit to yourselves that you secretly liked it, ...hopefully you'll do it the following week, and if not the following week, then the following month.

Here is where you can do your part. Invite a friend or two and show them the beauty of a Positive Judaism. Maybe you will influence them to try it in their own lives as well. Think of the impact you can have in the lives of your fellow Jews. Think of how you can do your small part in instilling a positive, joyful brand of Judaism in someone else's life.

In addition, Judaism requires action, not just belief. This is why we should think about what it means to be actively Jewish, rather than being passively Jewish. These actions can vary. They can be social justice projects, like feeding the poor, or housing the homeless. They can be measures which support the community, such as attending a minyan, or joining a synagogue or other Jewish institutions. They can even be as simple, or as complex, as study and learning.

I truly believe much of the frustration of those who want to be more actively Jewish is centered around not quite knowing what to do, or how to go about doing it; how to have a meaningful and positive Shabbat dinner at home, for example. It's the frustration of figuring out how to put these ideas and desires into action.

If you fall into this category, let me offer some advice. Follow my first rule of research - Ask Someone Who Knows! As Pirkei Avot says, "Aseh lecha rav." Find yourself a teacher. It doesn't have to be a rabbi. It can be anyone who is willing to help a fellow Jew in their quest. Pick up the phone. Or send an e-mail. But don't keep it to yourselves.

I will let you in on a little secret. Judaism is not for the Rabbi alone, or the Cantor alone, or the Board alone, or for the children alone. Judaism is for all of us. The synagogue, a congregation, does not belong to any one person or group either. It also belongs to all of us. It exists to serve our needs, whether those needs are spiritual, social or educational. The synagogue is the focal point of Jewish life and must remain so whether one comes every day or comes once a year. A synagogue is an oasis for the world, not from the world. The synagogue is the first step toward creating a positive Jewish experience.

Furthermore, in my concept of a Positive Judaism, there is no room whatsoever for guilt, because guilt is not a Jewish concept. Guilt might make you attend a service or do something "Jewish" every now and then, but it certainly will not keep you engaged. It is certainly no way to get your children or grandchildren interested, involved, and engaged either.

To put it another way - Judaism should not be about "OY." It should be about JOY! We must put the "J" back in Judaism. Judaism is about life and celebration, not asceticism. I applaud anyone who is dissatisfied in the sense he or she would like to be more actively Jewish, more participatory. I applaud anyone who, instead of seeing Judaism as abstract principles which are fine for discussion, want to absorb those principles and incorporate them into their lives. Being part of a community dedicated to a way of life, with like minded people who feel the same way, gives us a sense of meaning and purpose, belonging and friendship. This is Positive Judaism.

Joy and creativity. "Ivdu Et Hashem B'simcha." Worship God With Joy. This is my motto. It's the outlook on life we should have as we go about our daily lives.

A positive Judaism is all about joy and gladness, with a little common sense thrown in as well. A sense of finding positive reasons to belong to a synagogue, and to be actively Jewish. It's not about changing Judaism. It's about changing our perception of Judaism. It's about digging down into the well of Judaism and coming out with those buckets of water that we need to sustain and nourish our lives. We might each bring out a different bucket of water, but we must at least go to that well and take out some water.

The goal of Positive Judaism is to keep Judaism alive, to keep our synagogues thriving, and to make sure there is a viable Judaism for our children and grandchildren. We must continue to lead engaged Jewish lives. While we each do so in our own ways, we must understand that it's a lifestyle we must never give up or do without. It is why we must continue to engage in this dialogue, think about and put into action, ways of drawing in ourselves, our families and our friends.

Hopefully, by stressing this type of Positive Judaism, by seeing all the good, joy and pleasure we can have by living this kind of life, we will be able to keep Judaism as a vital and thriving force, not only in our own lives, but in the lives of our families and friends as well.

Shemitism

2

W e're all familiar with the term anti-Semitism. For a number of reasons it is defined as the hatred of Jews. Semites, although it technically includes Arabs, is a term used to refer to the Jewish people, because we, the descendants of Judah, hence the name Jews, and Abraham, the first Jew, are also the descendants of Noah's son Shem. Who was Shem, and what made him worthy of, in essence, having the Jewish people named after him?

In the interest of full disclosure, please note that Shem is my favorite biblical character, which is why I wrote my Master's Thesis about him (there's nothing like doing scholarly research on an obscure figure whose life story exists solely in the rabbinic imagination). I even went off on a wild goose chase to find his purported burial place in Tzefat!

Why do I find Shem so interesting? Because, legend has it, Shem, along with his great-grandson Ever, started the world's first Yeshivah. Among their students were Abraham, Isaac and Jacob (and Hammurabi). Now this legend, this Midrash, is quite far-fetched. It states that Shem possessed the Torah hundreds of years before Mount Sinai and actually taught that Torah to the Patriarchs. What is interesting about this Midrash, is not so much that it defies logic and the text of the Torah itself, but the way in which the concept, that there was such a Yeshivah, has been interpreted over the years.

This interpretation teaches us that if we emulate Shem, if we are true Semites, we realize there is not only one way of being Jewish, of being God-like, or of being a good Jew. Rather, Shem teaches us that depending on our individual circumstances, on the world and society around us, and its influences upon us, we might have to take different approaches to God and Judaism. We learn there are many ways, not only one true and valid way, of being worthy descendants of Shem, of being a true Jew, and a true Semite.

Shem was chosen by God to be the namesake of the Semites and the Jewish people for all time for a number of reasons. First, before the flood, Shem grew up in a world filled with corruption, or as the Torah calls it, Hamas. Nevertheless, he refused to follow those ways or succumb to the temptations of the day. Second, when Noah planted a vineyard and got drunk, it was Shem and his brother Japheth who took a blanket and covered their naked father. This incident might be viewed as the first "mitzvah" performed in the Torah. Certainly it was the first example of "Kibbud Av Va'em," honoring one's parents. This is why, for the rabbis, Shem's willingness to perform this mitzvah, the initiative he took and the zeal he demonstrated, meant that Shem exhibited the character traits of honoring one's parents and sexual modesty, and was therefore worthy of teaching these qualities to others.

However, Shem did more than that. Shem taught important values to our patriarchs, values that he, having lived in such a dangerous time, realized the patriarchs must know and understand in order to survive as Jews in their world. We too must learn and heed the lessons Shem taught the patriarchs, because they are what we need to live as Jews in our world; the important characteristics one needs as a Jew in order to live and survive in any age.

What were these lessons and values? Abraham's mission was to convince his neighbors of the one true God. He needed to learn how to reach out to people, especially the polytheists; and how to inspire them to bring them closer to God. Abraham learned these traits at Shem's Yeshivah. From this we learn that one way to be a Semite is to be kind and hospitable, and bring people closer to God.

Isaac, on the other hand, was known for different characteristics. He was a man who neither left the study hall, nor did he ever leave the Land of Israel. Isaac devoted himself to Torah study and to the worship of God. This too is a particular way which Jews today, Semites, can express their Judaism. Isaac's way is also valid, because making sure the heritage of our ancestors is passed on to our children, is an important component of being Jewish.

Jacob, however, was the real beneficiary of Shem's teachings, and the one patriarch whose course of study is most relevant today. Jacob had to live and conduct business among strangers and non-Jews. Thus, he needed extra time, fourteen years in fact, studying with Shem before going to live with his Uncle Laban. Just like Jacob had to learn how to live in the outside world, the "real world," so do Jews today have to learn how to live in a secular, often corrupt, and often anti-Semitic society. We must learn to act like Jacob by maintaining our Jewish identity and values, even when living in a society or culture where it is difficult to do so.

Being a descendant of Shem means acting like Shem in terms of modesty and respect, as well as in terms of teaching and learning, whether it's kindness like Abraham, Godliness and Torah like Isaac, or the ways of the world and maintaining our Jewish identities and values, like Jacob.

In the Yeshiva of Shem and Ever we encountered a model of Judaism which said that while we must always teach Torah, God and Israel, that is not always enough. Rather, there are many ways we can learn and live by the Torah. We just need to find the ways which work best for us at our particular time and place. This is the ultimate lesson and curriculum of the Yeshivah of Shem and Ever. As descendants of Shem we are called Semites precisely because we take these lessons to heart.

Whether our path to God is like that of Shem, or like that of Abraham, Isaac, or Jacob, we can find and follow our path, always be a Semite, and always take the lessons of the Yeshivah of Shem and Ever to heart.

FIFTEEN MINUTES OF WISDOM

3

It is commonly understood that the generation which built the Tower of Babel did so because they wanted to reach the heavens; to reach God. However, God thwarted their plan by changing their languages so that they couldn't communicate with each other, before scattering them all over the Earth.

Why did God do that? What was so wrong about building a Tower? Aren't we better off as a society if we share a common purpose and if we speak the same language? Shouldn't we be celebrating the fact, especially given the situation in the world today, that hundreds, or perhaps even thousands of people saw fit to work together to build something lasting?

Yes we should. However, the reason that God thwarted their plan was because our commonly understood reason isn't the true reason the people had for building that Tower. The truth is those people, that society, built the Tower because

237

they wanted to make a name for themselves. They wanted, not wealth, not the ability to be God-like, but rather they wanted.... Fame.

I say this because that is what the Torah explicitly tells us was the motivation. The people said to one another, ""Hava nivei lanu," let us build for ourselves, and "Naaseh Lanu Shem," and we will make for ourselves a name. In other words, the society which built the Tower of Babel, which first got together to work collectively towards a common goal, disintegrated over a clash of egos and a desire for fame and attention.

While the people started out with a common goal and purpose, as they built the Tower they lost sight of that goal and purpose. As they reached towards the sky, the builders made sure it was known that their Tower was for them and them alone, for the purpose of making for themselves a great name. They lost whatever connection they had, whatever they previously might have felt for their friends and neighbors or for anybody else who was not involved in the building of the Tower. In its place came jealousy, hatred, selfishness and self-interest as they argued over who could become the greater builder and whose role was more important. God changed their language and scattered them because of their desire for fame, because of their egos, not because of their desire to reach God and to be God-like.

Was their fifteen minutes of fame worth it? No, it wasn't. As we learn, fame should not be our goal. God wants us to reach Him and He certainly wants us to be more like Him. That is why we are created in His image. However, God also wants us to do so in the right way; by building a society which is caring and sharing; a society where people work together for common goals; a society where fame and ego take a back seat to helping others; and a society where obtaining wisdom and using it properly should be our goal.

Seeking fame, even if only for fifteen minutes, has never been a Jewish value. However, obtaining wisdom, even if it only lasts for fifteen minutes, has been a Jewish value for thousands of years. By asking questions, by seeking to obtain wisdom, we can continue to learn, to grow, and to change. In the words of Ahad HaAm, the famous Zionist writer, "Learning, learning, learning: that is the secret of our survival."

Our goal and our purpose in life, has never been, nor is it now, to achieve fifteen minutes of fame. Rather, if we are indeed fortunate enough, it should be to achieve at least fifteen minutes of wisdom.

EDJEWCATION   4

As Jews, our knowledge, our learning, and our ability to adapt and be creative, have enabled us to survive as a people for thousands of years. Our adaptability has enabled us to overcome obstacles and persecutions, all while other civilizations have vanished. Today, Judaism is at a crossroads because far too many of us Jews, the so called People of the Book, have forgotten, or do not know, how to read the book. To remain Jewish, and to ensure a future for Judaism, we must be better educated about our religion and our faith, because education, learning, and knowledge, are, and have always been, the keys to our survival as a people.

We all know that the word educated is spelled E-D-U-C-A-T-E-D. Today, however, we have to do our part to become better ED-JEW-CATED. We can only become more EdJEWcated by making the effort to do so. And if we make that effort, if we take the time, we will see that Jewish learning can be stimulating, fun and meaningful to our lives.

Becoming better EdJEWcated does not mean having to sit in on boring lectures or memorize rituals and facts by rote. It does mean using our spare time reading, listening to or watching something that has Jewish content. We can read books on all facets of Jewish life, thirty seven thousand of which are on Amazon. We can read stories in the newspaper about Israel or about the Jewish community. We can surf the internet for websites containing information on anything and everything which interests us about Judaism. Today, more than ever, there are a myriad of opportunities to engage in Jewish learning, because technology has made Jewish learning so much more accessible. Anything that we do which connects us to Judaism and the Jewish people will make us better EdJEWcated, sometimes without even realizing that it's happening.

In a little-known passage from the Torah, Moses compares the Torah to a Well because like a well, the Torah is deep, plentiful, and never-ending. Jewish learning, EdJEWcation, is also like a Well. It too is deep, plentiful, and never-ending. Its water is always available and it's always accessible. We just have to be willing to come to it.

At first, this idea of being more EdJEWcated might frighten us. While we might be afraid to take too much from the Well, one of the strengths of Judaism is that we can come to this Well with whatever sized bucket we want to bring with us and take out as much or as little as we can handle. Start off with a small bucket. When we realize that we can carry the bucket, that we like the water, we can come back for more. Maybe with a bigger bucket. Or maybe we can reach down deeper into the well. No matter how we approach the well, the important thing is that we do in fact approach that well of Jewish learning and become better EdJEWcated.

This is Judaism. Something for everyone. You want to only take a little. Fine. You want to reach deeper and take more. Even better. As long as we keep in mind there will always be plenty there to nourish and sustain us.

Don't just go to the Well once and be satisfied. Return to that Well over and over again. Each time bring a bigger bucket. Each time reach a little deeper. Each time become more and better EdJEWcated. Then use the water it provides, the water of our Torah, the knowledge that we gain, to sustain, nourish and satisfy our Jewish lives.

There's the story of three men who find themselves on a sinking boat. One of the men was a hedonist; another was a pious gentile; the third was a Jew. As they realized that they had only minutes before their little vessel would sink into the deep waters, each man became busy.

The hedonist rushed about, looking desperately for his final source of pleasure–perhaps he could find a bottle of brandy or whiskey.

The pious gentile spent those precious, final minutes, praying fervently that he might be spared from hellfire and brimstone.

The Jewish passenger resolved to spend those minutes....... learning how to live underwater!

Hopefully, we will never find ourselves on a sinking boat or stuck underwater, but if God forbid we do, wouldn't it be satisfying to know that we have taken the time to edJEWcate ourselves how to survive? If we take the time to become as edJEWcated as we are educated ourselves, if we edJEWcate our children as much as we educate them, then we have done our part to sustain the continued survival and growth of the Jewish people.

THE FOUR SONS IN
THE 21ST CENTURY

5

Judaism doesn't shy away from questions, which is one reason why the Passover Seder is the ultimate pedagogical tool. The Seder is an opportunity, over a meal, to retell our history to each new generation, in the hope that they will come to understand and appreciate our heritage and pass it on to the next generation. The words, prayers, and stories of the Haggadah remind us of our obligation to question, not only why is this night different, but other aspects of our religion as well.

As Jews, we believe it is by questioning and learning that we can truly appreciate the truth and beauty of the Torah and of Judaism. We indoctrinate our children with the idea that not only is it permissible to ask questions, but it is required of them to do so. Hopefully, our answers will not only satisfy them, but make them want to ask more and learn more.

One aspect of the Haggadah does just that; the passage about the Four Sons. Who are these four sons? Reading the passage literally, it is about four specific children. One is wise, one is wicked, one is simple, and one doesn't know how to ask. On the other hand, we can read this passage metaphorically or symbolically, the way it was meant to be read. These four sons represent four different types of Jews, which is why we must relate the story of the Exodus to them in a way they are able to understand; a way they will be able to see themselves as being part of the experience.

Working backwards, we begin with The One Who Doesn't Know How to Ask. Not only does he not know how to ask, he doesn't know what to ask, why to ask, when to ask, or that he's even allowed to ask. This is the Jew who doesn't know where to begin. To this Jew we much reach out, we must encourage him or her to ask, and then, most importantly, we must answer with patience and understanding. That is how we bring him or her back into the fold and hope that we have created a spark of hunger for more.

Next is The Simple Son. He has some knowledge and schooling but he doesn't ask questions. He knows that he has to have a Seder and he knows the rituals. He performs them as a matter of course but doesn't know why he's even doing it. This is the child who is taught in Hebrew School what to do, but not necessarily how to do it or why it's being done. His Jewish education might have stopped after Bar Mitzvah so that just as his mind grows, as his capacity for understanding grows, his knowledge of Judaism becomes stagnant or recedes. He is satisfied that he knows how to do everything and doesn't need to know any more, doesn't need to learn and doesn't need to grow more in his Judaism. This is the Judaism of a child, not the Judaism of an adult. We have to show this person there is more to Judaism than what he realizes; more than what he learned in Hebrew School or as a child. We need to show him the benefits of an adult Judaism, and how much more he can get out of it if only he takes the time and makes an effort.

The Wicked Son is really a misnomer. Publix Supermarkets in Florida prints Haggadahs with very nice pictures in them. In the Publix version, the Wicked Son doesn't look all that wicked. He looks more smug and disinterested. Cynical is another word that comes to mind. He is the Jew who performed all the rituals and asked all the questions at some point in his life but he is or has never been satisfied with the answers. And so he smirks. However, the fact that the he's still here, still having a Seder, means that he's still interested. It means that he's still searching for answers. He's still learning. He just won't admit it. Many Jews fall into this category. Instead of turning them away we should encourage and praise them for their effort and interest. We should tell them that it's good to be cynical and it's good to question. It is even a religious requirement going back to the days of Abraham.

Finally, there is The Wise Son. The true wise son is the one who has been one of the other three sons at some point in his or her life. He has gone through the stages and has asked the questions. He has gotten answers, studied, continues to study, and is now even beginning to share that knowledge with others. We hope and pray that the other three sons eventually turn into this wise son.

Wise doesn't mean genius. It doesn't even mean observant. It means someone who understands that study and questioning are important parts of Judaism. He knows there are many questions and possibly many answers. He knows he is free to believe and practice his Judaism as it was intended; by learning and studying, sometimes for its own sake, sometimes to increase practice or observance, but always by questioning, learning and growing, both as a person and as a Jew.

Although we are familiar with the names of these four sons given to them by the Haggadah, we can also give them different, more modern names; names that reflect the reality of Jewish life today, in the twenty-first century. Instead of wise, wicked, simple, and mute, we can call them committed (wise), uncommitted (wicked), unaffiliated (simple), and assimilated (doesn't know how to ask). The descriptions above still apply, only now we see these people for where they really fit into the fabric of modern Jewish life.

Despite the fact that the Seder is the most attended Jewish ritual observance, there are still many Jews who have no interest and no inclination to attend a Seder or do anything else that is "Jewish." Not only is this truly unfortunate, but it is also dangerous for our survival as a people. Therefore it is up to us to open up the discussion to bring the uncommitted, the unaffiliated, and the assimilated back into the fold.

While the Seder is the perfect opportunity to do so, any time Jews gather is an opportunity to share with our family and friends our positive Jewish experiences, to answer their questions, and to make them want to come back for more. Our goal should be to emulate the wise son; to not only ask questions, but through our interest and study, be able to answer the questions of others, and to encourage others to become more involved in their Judaism. We do so in order that one day, all Jews will not only participate in a Seder, but the uncommitted Jew becomes committed, the unaffiliated Jew affiliates, the assimilated Jew comes back, and that together, as a Klal Yisrael, we all become Wise.

A DAILY SEDER 6

Passover! After the first two nights, what is really left of the holiday? Why do we still need to observe Passover beyond the Seders? It can't be just to remember the Exodus. We are commanded to do that every day, not just on Passover. So what is the purpose of celebrating Passover for seven days, or eight days in the Diaspora?

I'll answer this question by posing another. Have you ever had a third night Seder? The very thought of another Seder is ridiculous. One Seder is enough. Two is more than enough. Why would anyone want more? As silly as it may sound, the idea of more Seders might actually be a good thing for the Jewish commu.... and religion. Just because there are no more Seders doesn't mean that we stop observing the holiday after they're concluded. In other words, don't think that Passover is "over" when the Seders are done, and it's goodbye until the next big event, Rosh Hashanah!

Jews are drawn to the Seder, the primary observance of Passover. Jews gather for Seders with family and community in numbers that are quite remarkable. According to recent studies, seventy five percent of Jews have some sort of Seder, even if it's only a family dinner that they call a Seder. The Seder is the most observed Jewish ritual, followed by the lighting of Hanukkah candles.

But in this age of individualism, for one or two nights anyway, we all become part of a community. We forget about our individual needs and focus on our families, friends, guests and even strangers. We celebrate this holiday together.

While many Jews stay home by themselves on the High Holidays, on Passover they at least invite others or are invited by others into their homes where they observe and dine together. That single commandment instructing every generation of Jews to tell the story of redemption from Egypt brings Jews together. Even if only for a night or two, we move away from our aloneness into an encounter with one another and our tradition at our Seder tables.

In the Torah we are instructed, "V'hee-gad'ta l'vinkhah," "And you shall tell your child on that day." This commandment has inspired every generation of Jews to connect the telling of the ancient liberation from slavery to a search for understanding of the meaning of freedom in a contemporary context.

The great sage Hillel says in Pirkei Avot, "Do not separate yourself from the community." Perhaps he had Passover in mind when he said it, because what happens after the Seders are over? We go back to our lives as individuals. We separate ourselves from the family, friends and communities which we were just a part of. We convince ourselves that it is better and easier to be alone. That way we can make or break all the rules we want. But the fact that Passover is a weeklong celebration culminating with a seventh day holiday teaches us that the community feeling that we enjoyed that first and second night should not be extinguished just because there is no formal Seder the rest of the week.

Every night during the Passover holiday can be an occasion for a Seder. It doesn't need to be the Seder of the Haggadah; it doesn't need to be the Seder of the four cups of wine, and afikomen, and bitter herbs; or even a huge meal! But it is, and can be, a Seder of family, of friends, and of community. It can, and must, be another opportunity to get together with fellow Jews over leftovers (and let's face it, who doesn't have leftovers after the Seder) to maybe talk about how our particular Seders went, or to talk about any other topic of interest.

A number of years ago I actually had a seventh night Seder because our tradition tells us that on the seventh day of Passover the Israelites crossed the Red Sea. So we drank four cups of water instead of wine and discussed the Miracle at the Sea instead of the four sons.

We can talk about Miriam's cup, current events, Israel, or Judaism in general. We can talk about any of the topics that we didn't get to on the first two nights because of time constraints. Or we can talk about anything that is on our minds. The idea is to at least get together and talk because the seven days of Passover present us with the opportunity, since we can't go anywhere else, to reconnect with our family, friends, and community. If Shemini Atzeret is God's way of saying, stay and spend an extra day with me, then the last six days of Passover are God's way of saying, spend an extra day with your family and friends.

The Seder teaches us many lessons. These lessons should not only be remembered and acted upon only once or twice each year. We read "ha lachma anya," Let all who are hungry come and eat. Shouldn't we adhere to this all year round by inviting people, whether they be friends or strangers, to come and dine with us? We read the four questions. We read "You shall teach your children." Can't we do that all year round? Can't we gather at any time during the year and ask questions about why we as Jews observe Shabbat? Can't we gather every week over a Shabbat dinner for example, and engage in a Shabbat Seder, a discussion about what Shabbat means?

We can do it on Shabbat. We can do it anytime. We can do it with family and friends. We can do it with strangers. We can share it with our community. We don't have to limit the joy of the Seder experience to only one or two nights each year. We can do it the whole week. We can do it anytime during the year. Not as a burden, but as a sign of joy and celebration, and family, friends and community.

A Two Minute
Elevator Ride

7

We live in an age where tweeting rules; where we sum up our lives in status updates of one hundred and forty characters or less. We live in the age of media sound bites and advertising slogans. However Judaism has never been like that. It has always been more and required more. We understand that Judaism, prayer, God, and perhaps even most importantly, support for Israel, cannot be summed up in a sound bite, or a tweet, or a slogan.

Unfortunately, not everyone shares this same understanding. They want their Judaism delivered in the same manner and with the same message they receive all the other data in their lives. Short; quick; to the point; and certainly not taxing anyone's attention span. The question then is, how can we make Judaism fit into this modern mode of delivery without sacrificing its essential message and elements?

A debate was held some time ago in New York between Rabbi Daniel Gordis and Professor Peter Beinart on the future of Israel. They disagreed on many topics but there is one thing they agreed on. A question was asked, "Both of you have written about the tragedy of young American Jews who have no connection to Judaism and the fate of the Jewish state. So let's say you were stuck in an elevator with one of the people from that demographic and you had two minutes to sell them on why they should re-engage with Jewishness and Zionism and the Jewish people. What would you say?"

Gordis answered first and said that the question is illegitimate and he wouldn't answer it. You can't explain Judaism or Israel in two minutes because it's too complicated and takes years of study to truly understand. Beinart agreed with Gordis saying that it's too late to give anyone who asks that question an answer because we've already failed them and it's too late in the game to make it up.

Both of these educated men, who presumably care about Judaism and Israel, and how to engage younger Jews especially, took the position that the question was baseless and they wouldn't answer it. I respectfully disagree with both Gordis and Beinart. Here's why.

It's true that we can't sum up the case for Israel in a two minute sound bite and we can't fight media distortion and inaccuracies with catchy slogans. No, we can't explain why someone should be Jewish during the course of an elevator ride. At the same time we can't dismiss the questioner or the question either. We can't afford to alienate anyone who legitimately shows some interest in these questions; someone we need on our side.

This is why we need to look for a hook to get them in. We have that hook! It's called the Torah. It tells us that we all stood at the foot of Mount Sinai and heard God's voice as he delivered the Ten Commandments. That's right, the Ten Commandments! We didn't stand there and listen to all six hundred thirteen at once. We didn't receive the oral law at that time; the Mishnah and the Talmud. No. All we got were ten!

The reason all we received at the time was ten was because we didn't have the attention span. We only had the attention span, even for God, to listen to Ten Commandments. God knew what we were capable of and that is why he started with ten. The people's response? "Naaseh V'nishma" - We will do and we will listen. We will listen for more.

The great sage Hillel also understood our capacity to absorb information. Many years later, when asked by the potential convert to explain the Torah while standing on one foot, Hillel famously replied; "What is hateful to you, do not do unto your neighbor. This is the entire Torah. The rest is commentary. Now go and study!"

Rabbi Gordis used this particular example to say that Hillel was wrong in his answer to the convert because just like the elevator question, the request was illegitimate and not worthy of a response. But I believe that Hillel was right. He understood the essential nature of the request and in the process had the foresight to provide us with an answer when asked that question today.

Only today we have to give that answer a bit differently. Today we can't just send the convert away, or in this case, the fellow Jew away and say, go study. The reason is that they can't study. They don't know how to study. Besides, study is too time consuming. They just want the answer, as simply as possible, and then want to go on their way. That is why today's response must be, "What is hateful to you, do not do unto your neighbor. This is the entire Torah. The rest is commentary. Give me your number and I'll text you.

Yes, I'll text you. Text messaging. That is what this must be about. Our history. Our texts. The average Jew doesn't know how to find these texts and probably doesn't even know that they exist or what's in them. That is why it is incumbent upon us to provide them. Not all at once. But one at a time. And then we must engage in a continuing dialogue with that person.

We begin by sharing with them some of our texts, which explain the importance of Israel, for example. We engage them by answering their questions, openly and honestly. We keep them interested by sharing our Judaism, our way of life, with them. This is the only way to succeed. This is the only way to make sure that that elevator ride is meaningful. We ask for their number and promise to keep in touch.

This is what God told us on Mount Sinai. Moses will also be coming up in the elevator. Yes it's a forty day ride, not a two minute ride. However, if you stay in touch, if you wait for him to come back, if you wait for My next text, you won't be disappointed.

It is also why, although we refer to the Ten Commandments as the Decalogue - Latin for ten sayings - the truth is that the Ten Commandments, is really all about dialogue. God began it on Mount Sinai. It is up to us to continue, especially with those who need our guidance the most. And if all we can spare is two minutes in an elevator, we should take advantage of what those two minutes offer us, and never turn down the opportunity to engage a fellow Jew in living a Jewish life.

PART VII

A FULFILLING JEWISH LIFE

HAVING A VISION 1

s mentioned in the previous chapter, we live in an interesting age, an age where technology rules; an age where everyone is connected to everyone else through the computer, through e-mail, blogs, iphones, Facebook, and Twitter. However technology cannot be the end all and be all of our existence. We require more. We require much more depth. We require that our religion, for example, be able to engage us and sustain us; our entire beings; our hearts, our minds and our souls. If all we care about is a Jewish version of Twitter, then our prayers can be summed up as follows:

"I'm sorry God. I've sinned. I've been bad. I promise not to do it again. I'll change. I'll be good. I promise I will. Please forgive me, ok?"

Perfect - Exactly 140 characters. The Twitter limit.

Having established that we could do in one hundred forty characters what it takes us days and countless hours to do, especially over the High Holiday season, why don't we just all say that one line, and then go out and enjoy the rest of the day?

The reason is because asking God for forgiveness doesn't just come three days a year. It actually comes three times a day. In the daily amidah, recited three times each day, we have the prayer, "Slach Lanu Avinu Ki Chatanu, M'chal Lanu Malkeinu Ki Pashanu, Ki El Mochel V'soleach Attah." Forgive us our father for we have sinned, pardon us our King for we have transgressed, because you are a merciful and forgiving God.

Again under the Twitter limit. Perfect.

We have summed up hours of prayer in one short sentence. Say it every day, three times a day, and we should be satisfied that God has forgiven us.

However, if this is all we get out of services, we would come away feeling empty; that something was missing. We really don't want to come to a synagogue for just one sentence. Having realized this, perhaps we might also begin to understand how and why Judaism, prayer, God, the High Holidays, and yes, even the case for Israel, cannot be summed up in a sound bite or a tweet. We might begin to realize that our prayers and the focus on forgiveness need to be repeated in order to get us to really concentrate on it and engage it.

In so doing, by spending more time, by becoming more engaged, we come to see it's not enough that we ask God to forgive us or confess our sins to Him. No. God wants us to do something else. God wants us to tell Him what we are going to do this year that is different, and better than what we did last year. We say to God, yes, if You forgive me, not only do I promise not to repeat the bad behavior, but I also promise to change my behavior.

What do I mean by change our behavior? To make doing God's will, living by His Torah, an integral part of who we are. To come away with more than a sound bite or a tweet. To not only have a plan to change, but to have a vision to help you focus on getting there.

What is this vision? While each person might and should have their own vision, let me suggest one such vision which we might share together. It's not an original vision. I didn't make it up or think of it myself, but I believe that it's one we should all share. As the Prophet Isaiah implored us, we should each be an "Or Lagoyim" a light unto the nations, and make a difference in this world. We should be a light, be kind, and do good for others, so that others will come to emulate us.

Implementing Isaiah's vision means we recognize our obligations as Jews, and that Judaism, at its most basic level, is a religion that strives to do one thing and one thing only - to make us all mensches. This is why for the past thirty five hundred years Jews have been telling ourselves, our children, and the rest of the world five things. Be good. Be kind. Be honest. Be ethical. Be moral. How's that for a vision? How's that for a purpose?

Judaism teaches us that the most important thing is to do good, to do charity, and to refrain from saying bad things, refrain from engaging in lashon hara. We do these things, not just feel these things. Our purpose is to continually perform mitzvot, not mere random acts of kindness. Judaism tells us we must go out of our way to be kind, to be ethical, and to be moral. This is why mitzvah means commandment, not a good deed. It is why we don't help the little old lady across the street because we want to; we do it because we have to. We don't just do it once and pat ourselves on the back. We do it once to train ourselves to do it a second time; and then a third time. We do it because we are expected to be an "Or Lagoyim," and to lead by example. We do it to instill in us the conviction to make this behavior a routine part of our lives.

Stripped to its essence, Judaism is all about the commandment that we act with chesed and kindness to our fellow man, that we love our neighbor as we love ourselves. This is how we should live our lives; by doing any of the myriad of mitzvot which can be done if we just take the time to think about it, and then go out and do them. This is how we fulfill the vision of Isaiah to be an "Or Lagoyim."

We must all have the vision to partner with God to complete His work of creation and make the world a better place. However, we can only do so if we act with kindness and compassion to our fellow man. Start by being an "or," a light, to just one other person, because hopefully you ignite something in them and they ignite something in another, and so on and so on. It is the way we bring more light and less darkness into the world.

CIRCLES 2

What is it about the religion of Judaism that turns people off; makes them not want to live a Jewish life; or become less involved or less observant? Haven't we all heard from people we know, whether family or friends, grumblings as to why they don't come to shul or why they don't follow a certain practice, or why they've even given up on Judaism? I'm sure if we were to think about these issues we could probably form our own list as well.

Is it that we pray in a language we don't understand? Is it that we have too many rules and rituals such as Kashrut and observing Shabbat? Is it an emphasis on depressing holidays like Yom Kippur or on our history as a people? Is it the length of services; sitting in a synagogue for over two hours on a beautiful Saturday morning? Maybe it's reading from the Torah about an arcane set of practices that has absolutely no relevance to our lives today? Nevertheless, we still come and worship. We come to shul and participate in the service, despite these so called turn-offs. That is because there are more turn-ons, more reasons to come, and more and better reasons to be Jewish, than there are turn-offs, reasons not to come, and not to be Jewish.

Despite our reasons for coming, for participating, or for being involved, we can't ignore the numerous reasons and excuses people have for staying away. One such reason is that we tend to look at Judaism not as a holistic religion but by picking out the parts we like or we don't like. Unfortunately however, by picking and choosing, we whittle Judaism down to just parts. If the parts we don't like, the parts that keep us away, such as long services, or kashrut, outweigh the parts we do like, the friendship, the socialization, the big kiddushes, for example, then we say that Judaism as a whole isn't for us. However, we do a disservice to ourselves and to Judaism if we take the parts we don't like, and make those particular parts representative of the whole; thereby giving them an out-sized role in defining what Judaism is really all about.

The response to those who pick out one part they don't like as representative of all there is about Judaism, is that they're missing the point. The response is to ask them to ignore or not focus on what they don't like, but to look for the parts they do like instead. There are so many more of these to choose from. They might vary from person to person. But there is something in Judaism for everyone to like and want more from.

If we come across someone who is turned off to Judaism, we might want to ask them why, and have them point to a specific reason. Then we must counter with all the wonderful and beautiful things about Judaism that not only we like ourselves, but which they will like as well. Give them one to choose from and ask them to give it a chance. As I wrote in Positive Judaism, maybe it's Purim or Simchat Torah. Remind them that even if we don't like everything about Judaism, as a whole, you know what, it ain't too bad!

The opposite is also true. Those of us who participate do so because the positive aspects outweigh the negatives. But we also pick and choose what we like about Judaism and lose sight of the fact that Judaism is a whole, and that we too shouldn't ignore the parts we either don't like or are not as yet comfortable with.

If we focus more on the whole, in so doing we expand our Jewish horizons. We shouldn't just be satisfied if we come to Saturday morning services; we should try to come on a Friday night as well. Or try a weekday minyan on occasion. As I explain to those who are relative newcomers but who want to become regulars, "Don't worry if you can't follow everything. Rome wasn't built in a day. Follow what you can. Understand what you can. Ask. And then come back. You'll be amazed how it all will become so familiar."

If we're satisfied because we can understand the service, why not try understanding Jewish texts. Expand your reading list to include Jewish books. Come to a class. We're satisfied that we give tzedakah? Do tzedakah! Volunteer your time, whether it's for the shul or for any other worthy charitable or community organization. In other words, do a mitzvah or two.

Imagine a number of circles, each one representing some aspect of Judaism - prayer, kashrut, study, ethics, mitzvot. The number of circles is endless. If we belong to one circle, why not try belonging to two? If two, why not three? Maybe we try connecting the circle we're in to a circle next to it that we didn't choose and get into that circle. By doing so, if you can imagine, these circles will all begin to move together, interconnecting with each other. Hopefully you can see how these circles, these parts of Judaism, are really all part of one big circle.

It's up to us to make those circles come together. It is up to us to make our own circles bigger. It is up to us to include others in our circles and to do our best to show others how to use their circles. This is how we focus on what's good and positive about Judaism and not what we don't like about it. It is a way of looking beyond the minutiae in order to see the greater whole; because the whole is certainly greater than the sum of its parts.

Pirkei Avot, Ethics of Our Fathers, famously stated that the world rests on three pillars, Torah - the study of Torah; Avodah - service; and Gemilut Chasadim - acts of loving-kindness. It's not just one pillar which makes a complete Jew or a complete religion. It's all three. They are each in their own circle but only when the circles intersect and combine, only when we manage to be involved in all three, are we really on the road towards doing God's will.

Judaism is not just about the ordinary and comfortable. Sometimes we have to expand our Jewish horizons. Judaism not only rests on three pillars, but on the many circles and parts which forge together to create that one whole Judaism through which, and by which, we can all be proud to call our own.

Israel At Sixty-Four 3

In 2013, Israel will reach an important milestone. She will turn sixty-five. She therefore becomes eligible for Medicare and Social Security! There is something significant about turning sixty-five even if I'm going to use an American analogy. At sixty-five you are considered to be a senior citizen. You are no longer a child, an adolescent, a teenager, a young adult, or even middle aged. No. You are now old and presumably wise.

In thinking of Israel today, as it nears sixty-five, I realize why Israel is having such problems. No, not with her Arab enemies, but with Jews, especially American Jews, and younger American Jews; Jews who were not alive in 1948 and Jews who weren't even alive in 1967. In other words, Jews who only know Israel as it exists now; as a senior citizen.

There is a generation gap between younger Jews and those who have lived long enough to remember what it was like for Jews in America, for Jews anywhere in the world, before there was a State of Israel. These differences can best be summed up by an old Beatles song, "Will you still need me, will you still feed me, When I'm sixty-four?"

Do we still need Israel at sixty-four? Do we still support Israel at sixty-four? These are the questions being asked today among American Jews. Why support Israel? Why care about Israel? The answer is an easy "I don't know," especially because Israel is portrayed in the media as the bad guy, the bully, the occupier, the violator of human rights!

There is another reason for this generational divide over Israel, one that strikes at the heart of the problem. A recent book, by Professor Peter Beinart, called "The Crisis of Zionism,' has received a lot of attention for its criticism of Israel. However, who is actually facing this crisis and why is there a crisis? The crisis that Beinart refers to isn't taking place in Israel. It's taking place in America. It's taking place among those American Jews who have their own definition of Zionism, which is seemingly at odds with the policies or definition of Zionism espoused by the Israeli government. This difference is highlighted by how these Jews see, not just Israel, but see Judaism as well.

To younger Americans, Jews and non-Jews alike, reared with Western values, raised in a multi-cultural society, Zionism is not necessary. In fact Judaism is not necessary. According to this worldview, universalism is the goal, the way to live. Not tribalism. Not exceptionalism. Judaism merely sets Jews apart. Zionism sets Israel apart.

They say that all people should be able to live freely in Israel. Israel no longer needs to be a homeland for Jews. Jews no longer need a special homeland because we live as full, free citizens here in America! Some even advocate changing the words to Hatikva because it's too much about Jewish aspirations which are no longer necessary.

Why support a country at sixty-four or sixty five even? It's old. That was for my parents. It's not for me! That is the crux of the attitude which is so widespread today. To this I have a simple response. Many responses actually.

First. Germany. This was the same response we heard from German Jews for nearly a century. They were assimilated. They were cultured. They reached the highest levels of society. They too saw no reason to be "separated" as Jews. And then 1933 came. And 1935. And 1939. You know the rest.

The simple truth is that as safe and comfortable as we may feel, whether here in America or elsewhere, we will always be Jews. There will always be those who do not like us. If something horrific were to happen to us, what should we do then? Where should we go? Where can we go?

The one true crucial ideal of Israel, the one true promise of Israel, one that has lasted for sixty-four years, is that only with a Jewish State of Israel, can all Jews have a safe refuge. Only with a Jewish State of Israel, can all Jews have a home. Only a strong Jewish State of Israel will stand ready, willing and able to defend the Jewish people, wherever they may be.

Second. In our efforts to spread multi-culturalism, diversity, equality, and universalism we have lost sight of our history. We need to remind ourselves of that history. We need to remind our children and grandchildren. We need to speak to them and teach them our history. We need to tell them what it was like before 1948. Then, without being an alarmist, we need to impress upon them that, in the words of Rabbi

Daniel Gordis, "The Jews have a future because the Jews have a state." Then again, if you don't care about Jews having a future, then who cares about Jews having a state.

One of the problems is that for any Jew born after 1981, when Israel destroyed Iraq's nuclear reactor, other than inventing the cell phone, almost everything they have read or seen about Israel in the media is negative. They didn't witness 1948. They didn't witness the miracle of 1967. They weren't even alive for the raid on Entebbe or when Israel destroyed the Iraqi nuclear reactor. All they know and hear about is occupation and oppression and aggression.

This is why, when we speak to our children and grandchildren, we shouldn't just teach them ancient history, we should teach them modern history. We must show them what Israel is really like. We must impress upon them the advances made in science, technology, arts, and medicine. We must impress upon them all the good that Israel does. Show them. Teach them. Tell them the cell phone they can't live without was invented in... yes, in Israel. Point them to websites that show Israel in a positive light. Show them that Israel, while it may be ready to receive Social Security, is not ready to retire! It's still strong and it's still vibrant. However, it can only remain that way with our help and support.

The third response to this generational gap is a paraphrase of the television program, "Whose values is it anyway?" Those who criticize Israel, those who claim that Israel violates human rights, etc, do so based on one faulty premise. Yes, Israel is a democratic country, but it's Israeli democracy, it's Israeli Zionism, and it's Israeli values by which it must live and be governed. We make a very big mistake when we impose our version of American democracy and values onto Israel.

Americans, Jew and non-Jew alike, do not have to face what Israelis face on a daily basis. We're not worried about being attacked by Canada or Mexico. Who are we to impose our American version of the Bill of Rights, free speech, freedom of religion, etc, onto another country? The criticism of Israel we hear from many corners of the Jewish American spectrum is based on this faulty premise. You want to criticize free speech in Israel? What other country would tolerate members of its own legislature calling for its very destruction?

It is very easy to sit in the comfort, safety and freedom of America and criticize another country for not living up to, not their own ideals or laws, but our American ideals and laws. It's easy to do so when safety isn't one of our top priorities. It's easy to do so when we're not surrounded by enemies. It's very easy to ask someone else to live up to impossibly high moral and ethical standards while not demanding the same of oneself or one's own country. It's not as easy to praise and point out the positive.

It's much easier to criticize Israel and demand that Israel live up to these values rather than demand the same of Saudi Arabia, Syria, Egypt, or Iran. We only demand it of Israel because even at sixty-four, even as a senior citizen, Israel actually cares what others think; because even at sixty-four, Israel actually wants to do the right thing; wants to take the high moral and ethical ground. However, when after all these years, the other side still doesn't recognize our right to exist, we can't for a moment pretend that we can survive only with high minded ideals. We can't. No one can. Israel certainly can't and shouldn't be required to do so.

This is why Israel, in her own judgment, must be allowed to determine her own policies, as espoused by her democratically elected leaders. It is why Israel, in her own judgment, is best able to determine how to respond to terror and attacks. We cannot impose our idealistic American values on another democratic country. Rather, we must stand up for Jewish interests, stand up for Israel, and teach our younger generation that Israel, and the safety, security and future of the Jewish people must be a priority in our lives.

There is much that Professor Beinart writes with which I disagree. But to be fair, he did write something with which I wholeheartedly agree; a statement which sums up the problem and offers a solution; one to share with your children and grandchildren. Beinart writes, "I call the failure to give young American Jews the Jewish education necessary to live committed Jewish lives a "tragedy." I say that young American Jews need to care about Israel more than they care "about global warming, health care, gay rights, and a dozen other issues." We all need to care more about Israel!

Supporting Israel must be a part of our identity as Jews. The evangelical Christian community does a better job of educating their parishioners and getting them to support Israel than we do. That is because they see it as a religious obligation. We see it as just another political issue. Supporting Israel and standing up for her interests and her right to exist as a Jewish state is a religious requirement. Perhaps it is, or should be, the most important religious requirement we can have at the moment.

"Will you still need me, will you still feed me, When I'm sixty-four." The answer is YES. The answer must be YES.

EVANJEWLICAL 4

It's very easy and also quite silly to make ordinary words, which we use all the time in one context, into "Jewish" words when we want to use them in another context. An example is turning the word "terrified" into "Torahfied." What is "Torahfied?" It's the inability to remember one's lines when called to read from the Torah at one's Bar or Bat Mitzvah. There is however, one such word that we should consider not just using, but making it a part of our Jewish vocabulary.

We all know the word "Evangelical." An Evangelical refers to a Christian who is a believer in particular tenets of Christianity and who sometimes preaches the Gospel or tries to convert others to Christianity.

Can a Jew be an Evangelical? Of course not we would naturally say! How can a Jew preach the gospel or try to convert others to Christianity? Jews just don't do that. We have never been missionaries to non-Jews, and we have never gone out of our way to try to convert others. We haven't done so not only because it's not part of our religious requirements, and not only because we were prohibited from doing so by oppressive governments, but we haven't done so for one very good reason; the realization that we need to missionize to ourselves first. We need to bring our own back to Judaism, to show them what a Jewish life is all about, before we can begin to convert others.

We all need to become "EvanJEWlicals." We need to live Judaism, explain Judaism, and sell Judaism. No, not to non-Jews, but to our fellow Jews.

The High Holidays are about return. They are about looking inside ourselves and figuring out what we need to do in order to better ourselves. But we must also turn our attention outward rather than inward; to spend time taking what we have gained and learned and to share that with others. We must EvanJEWlicize to others. Now that we ourselves have hopefully returned, we must engage in the process of returning other Jews to their faith.

If you want to know how to do so, or if you're afraid of doing so, then take a lesson from the world's first EvanJEWlical - Abraham. To put it succinctly, Abraham made the people around him better. He elevated them. He did so by the way he led his life. He did so by showing hospitality and kindness.

When Abraham and Sarah left Haran for the journey to the Promised Land, they took with them, in the words of my favorite quote from the Torah, "V'et hanefesh asher asu b'Haran," "The people that they had made in Haran." This refers to all the people whose lives were changed and influenced under Abraham and Sarah's guidance. It refers to all the people who converted, if not to Judaism, or to Abraham's version of Judaism, then at least to monotheism.

The word "nefesh," can also be translated as souls. Abraham and Sarah made and transformed people's souls. Abraham made nefashot by the way he led his life; through hospitality and kindness. There were no scare tactics in Abraham's method, no harassment, no high pressure salesmanship. Just a simple, honest and kind way of life that people wanted to follow.

Today, we too can make nefashot just like Abraham did. And just like Abraham, we can do so without harassing others or pressuring them into doing things our way.

There's a midrash in the Talmud which explains how Abraham planted an "inn" in Beersheva, at a place where merchants would pass by. He invited them in and gave them food and drink. When these merchants, travelers or strangers would ask Abraham how they could repay him, Abraham didn't ask for money. He said, just don't forget to thank God, for He provided all this for you.

That was all it took. A little bit of hospitality and a simple acknowledgement of God. Nothing heavy-handed. Nothing which these people would be resentful of, or feel like they were tricked in some way, when they left. When these travelers saw that this was how a God fearing man behaved, they were naturally drawn to him. So they spoke to him, questioned him, broke bread with him, followed him, and then came to the conclusion that this is a man and a God they wanted to emulate.

Abraham was in the minority. He always was, as are we today. The Torah tells us that he had three hundred eighteen men who fought with him to rescue his nephew Lot against kings with mighty armies. Yet Abraham and his followers believed. And when they were successful, others, like the king of Shalem, broke bread with Abraham and praised the one true God. This is the mark of a successful EvanJEWlical.

We don't have to be on Abraham's spiritual level to be an EvanJEWlical. We don't even have to influence thousands or even hundreds. But we can be an EvanJEWlical by making even one person just a little more Jewish, by making one person do one more mitzvah, and by making one person join and come to synagogue.

Being an EvanJEWlical is not about trying to convert non-Jews to Judaism. It's about converting Jews to Judaism. It's about us, those of us who are involved, doing more, engaging in outreach, trying to influence others, and selling Judaism to our fellow Jews. It's doing so by behaving in a certain way. It's by not being afraid to say, "I'm Jewish; follow me. Do what I do." It's about being a role model. It's about showing that it's good to come to shul, to keep kosher, and to observe Shabbat.

What is it about Judaism that we're selling? It's a way of life. It's a value system. It's a community. It's working together for the common good. It's sharing and it's helping others. It's ethics and morals. And any good salesman will tell you that to sell something you must present it in a good light. In an optimistic light.

Despite our history, despite certain rituals and practices, Judaism is by nature a religion of optimism and joy. We must be happy to be in the company of our friends and fellow congregants who have come to share the experience with us. We can lift up our voices with joyous song, with excitement, and with pride in practicing and selling the beauty of our religion. That is something we can sell; something we can EvanJEWlicize about. That is something people will be interested in.

Coming to shul, being an involved Jew, should be seen as a joy. To learn, to pray, to socialize. And then share what you feel, what you enjoy, with others. That is how one becomes an EvanJEWlical. Every day is a celebration that we have the Torah, that we have such a rich heritage, that despite centuries of hardship and persecution we're still here, we're still practicing our religion, and doing so in a comfort and freedom that our ancestors would never have dreamed of.

God promised Abraham "I will bless those who bless you." As descendants of Abraham, as inheritors of that promise, we also receive these same blessings. We receive them by being like Abraham, and by being blessed by those whom we come in contact with. And they do so because we've shown them how to live like Abraham, how to be hospitable and kind, how to acknowledge God, and how to live a Jewish life.

We don't EvanJEWlicize because we feel we don't know enough to convince others, or because we are not worthy enough. We are all worthy of being EvanJEWlicals. We all have the ability to do so just by leading the lives we're leading and sharing it with our friends and family. It really is that simple.

Now is the time to look outward, beyond our own needs. Now is the time to look to others and sell Judaism to others. Now is the time for us to be EvanJEWlicals; to be salesmen for Judaism.

A BASEBALL YIZKOR 5

When we think of our loved ones who are no longer with us, our minds are filled with memories, the good and happy, as well as the sad and the melancholy. This is because our memories, our life experiences, and the influence of our loved ones, all serve to define us and make us who we are.

We all remember the people taken from us, too soon; people whom we still need and want. We need to hold on to those feelings and not erase them from our memory, because they are an important part of who we are.

We should reflect upon the fact that who we are has also been shaped by the happy moments in our lives, and by those simple moments that while not as momentous or life changing as births, weddings, and deaths, still have a profound impact on our memories.

If I were to ask what is Yizkor and how do we go about observing Yizkor, I'm sure the answer would be that Yizkor is a service, that it's a collection of specific prayers, and that we come to shul four times a year to recite these prayers.

On a certain level that answer is certainly correct, but it is also very simplistic. You see, if done properly, Yizkor is more than just coming four times a year, and it's more than just reciting particular prayers. True Yizkor can take many forms and can invoke many memories, hopefully pleasant ones, because if all we have are sad memories and not good and happy ones, believe me, we won't want to be saying Yizkor, because we won't want to be remembering.

So how do we go about doing Yizkor, instead of merely saying Yizkor? I believe it starts with the idea that we don't just remember that our loved ones have passed on. We must also specifically remember the moments that we shared with them, some private, some with other family members, some with friends, and some perhaps experiencing great historical and memorable occasions.

For example, as I wrote in an earlier chapter, we remember where we were, that July night in 1969, glued to our television sets, watching Neil Armstrong set foot on the moon. It was a historic moment. Who did you share that moment with? Who were you watching with? Who did you call on the telephone right afterwards?

Can you recall that moment today? Doesn't it bring back pleasant memories? Aren't you glad and grateful that you had people in your life to have shared that moment with? Can't you smile a little recalling that moment and envision the smiles of those you shared it with?

If we are talking about events from 1969, I can't help but remember a particular event which occurred in October of that year. The New York Mets won the World Series!

Certainly if you were from New York and rooted for the Mets you remember that World Series. It seems like ages ago and yet it seems like it was only yesterday. If you do remember that moment, or that season, do you remember who you shared it with? Parents, siblings, friends, children? Do you remember as a child spending an afternoon at the ballpark with your father perhaps; or with your siblings, or friends, or children?

And aren't these also happy memories, memories that help shape who we are?

I want to talk a little about baseball and the 1969 New York Mets not to be glib, but because baseball is a great metaphor for Yizkor, both in its simplicity and in the memories which it evokes. Like religion, among family, baseball can be a unifying force for good. It's something that can be shared with the whole family and whose memories can be passed down from generation to generation.

Did you ever see Babe Ruth play? Or maybe it was Joe DiMaggio or Willie Mays. Can you tell those stories to your children and grandchildren? Can you take your grandchild to a game and watch today's stars while telling him or her about yesterday's; the ones you idolized as a kid? Can you develop a bond, a closeness, which your grandchild will remember and then tell his or her children?

Can you envision a time where your child or grandchild, after you're gone, can turn to his child or grandchild and say, your great-grandfather took me to see Derek Jeter. Let me tell you about him. These are memories. This is how we make memories. Simple yet effective. That is Yizkor.

Returning to the 1969 Mets, I want to tell you that they performed their own Yizkor. It was something we can learn from.

Forty years after they won the World Series, most of the surviving members of the team got together for a reunion. Yes, they celebrated their remarkable achievement, but in the process they also reflected on their losses as well. In getting together with old teammates and friends, Tom Seaver, the Hall of Fame pitcher said "It is no doubt the highlight of my baseball life. Winning the World Series changes your life. There's a closeness that comes from it, you're kind of like brothers to your teammates. You have a much different relationship with them when you have that in common."

Getting together with those who are still alive, those you share a bond with, those you share memories with, is a Yizkor. It is especially true when you can stop and reflect that those memories and shared experiences are what makes you who you are.

Seaver went on, in words that are eerily reminiscent of what we do at Yizkor, "There will be a lot of laughs. Some tears, too," as he listed the names of players and coaches who have passed away since 1969, like Tommie Agee, Don Cardwell, Donn Clendenon, pitching coach Rube Walker, Tug McGraw, and of course the manager of that team, Gil Hodges.

"Most importantly, at the back of everybody's mind will be Gil," Seaver added. "He won't be there, but he will be there, you know?"

Isn't that what Yizkor is about? Highlights of your life, closeness to family and friends, shared memories? And by getting together for a reunion, whether it's a baseball team or a family, we share these memories, we reminisce, and we remember these events.

We laugh. And yes, we cry.

There's more to the Mets story. The Mets recently moved to a new ballpark, called Citifield. While there, those players noticed something, as did many of the fans. The new park paid homage to a lot of memories; but memories of the old Brooklyn Dodgers and New York Giants.

Where were the memories of the old Mets, they asked? They were not to be found. But they were needed, because those memories were also important, also part of whom they are.

The old players and the new fans complained to Mets management. Management listened and included more memories of the old Mets in the new ballpark.

We need a Yizkor when we come to the ballpark. We want our experience to not only be about the current team, and about the present, but we want it, and need it, to also be about our past. This because when we are in that environment, the ballpark, just like in shul, we need our Yizkor moment and our Yizkor experience. We need it so that we can share it with others who we bring to that game. Where we can sit and talk, and bond and reminisce, and share memories.

As we go through our lives, there are many places, many experiences, and many occasions which trigger our memories, and help us to recall our loved ones. We don't only need to be in shul for these memories to be triggered, and they don't only have to come four times a year. Anything can be a Yizkor. Our memories, both good and sad, are meant to be shared anytime we get together with our loved ones who are still here, who are still around to remember.

The actions we take in memory of our loved ones are our true Yizkors, not just our prayers. What we do with our memories, and how we express those memories to others, is significant, not the mere fact that we say, "I remember." It is why, when appropriate to do so, we must use every day as a Yizkor to our loved ones.

FINISHING OUR BOOKS 6

Books! We all own books, although today we don't read books, we read Nooks and Kindles! Perhaps the most famous book we have (aside from the Bible) is the Book of Life, which we pray God writes us in on the High Holidays. But there is another book that is not so well know. This is because it is a book we are still writing, both collectively and individually.

We're familiar with the words "Vayihee veen'soah ha'aron vayomer Moshe," "When the Ark was carried, Moses said..." We say them whenever the Torah is taken out of the Ark. And when the Torah is returned, we say "U'venucho yomar, shuvah Adonai revavot alphei Yisrael," "Return God the myriad of thousands of Israel," right before we sing the Etz Chayim. These prayers, are taken directly from the Torah.

What is unusual about these two verses is that they are enclosed, as if in parentheses, by the letter "Nun" written upside down on each side, in the Torah scroll.

According to the Talmud, these verses are enclosed by an inverted "Nun" because they form a separate book of the Bible! This view holds that there are really seven books in the Bible, not five. They are Genesis, Exodus, Leviticus, Numbers up to this point, these two verses, the remainder of Numbers, and Deuteronomy.

Why do these verses form their own book? At this point in the narrative, the Israelites were ready to begin their journey to the Promised Land, to Israel. The Torah had been received and the Tabernacle had been completed and consecrated. Moses believed they were ready, that the promise God made to our ancestors was about to be fulfilled.

But then something tragic happens. They don't go! And that is where these parenthetical verses appear.

The rabbis claim that these verses represent the book that was never written. This is the book relating to the conquest of the land of Israel by Moses; the book that should have been written, but wasn't. It wasn't, because of all the events that subsequently transpired.

Following these verses the Israelites complain about their food, Miriam and Aaron speak out against Moses, the spies report that the land will be impossible to conquer, Korach rebels against Moses, Moses strikes the rock, and so on. These incidents show that the Israelites were not ready to enter the Promised Land.

These two verses were written in parentheses to indicate to us that there's a break in the pre-ordained destiny of the Jewish people because of their actions. God left us a reminder with these parentheses what could have been, or more precisely, what should have been written in that book, but wasn't. These two verses represent a whole, complete book. We might call it the Book of the Destiny of the Jewish People.

Whatever we call it, and no matter how long or short it is, it is our duty to finish that book. To complete not only our own histories, but the history of the Jewish people. Each and every one of us has the ability to write that book, and to help fulfill our common destiny. Doing so doesn't necessarily require a tremendous amount of effort. If we have the ability to change another Jew's life, then we have the obligation to do so. If we have the opportunity to do our part to finish that book, then we have the obligation to do so. We have the obligation to not act as the individuals in the desert, but to act to foster a community in this oasis.

The book which remains to be written though is not our own individual books, our own life stories. Nor is it God's book; the one he seals on Yom Kippur. Rather, this book, which remains unwritten, is our story. The story of the Jewish people.

If we want to finish this book, we have to do it together, as a community. Writing this book is a joint project, a communal effort. It was individual greed and jealousy which prevented that biblical book from being completed. And it is that same individualism which is preventing it from being completed today.

The book is open. We have the chance to write it. We have the chance to finish it. We have the opportunity to truly shape the destiny of the Jewish people. The only question is, will we be the ones to finish it?

The final verse of this book, recited when we return the Torah to the Ark, states, "Shuvah Adonai Revavot Alphei

Yisrael" - Return God the myriad of thousands of Israel. The end of the book will thus be marked by the return of all Jews, everywhere - to the land of Israel, to the people of Israel, and to the God of Israel.

FOLLOW THE BLUE AND WHITE ROAD

7

There was a Broadway musical called Avenue Q which offered an interesting lesson in life. The lead character, Princeton (a puppet by the way), a recent college graduate, spends the entire show seeking his purpose; asking the deeper questions of life which haunt us all. Why am I here? Who am I? Where do I want to go? And how can I get there? Princeton learns in two hours what it might take most of us a lifetime to learn; that the search for purpose in life is not easy and requires us to engage in deep thought and action.

Ultimately, our purpose in life is connected to the journey we call life, a journey that we all share. Sometimes we share it together. Other times we go our separate ways. Purpose is another way of looking for something more out of life. Sometimes it's a way to find the easier path in life, or sometimes it's to reach a particular end.

In Judaism, in fact in many religions, this "purpose" has been transformed. We now call it "spirituality." We are seeking a spiritual purpose, as if by magic spirituality will lead us over the rainbow to that proverbial pot of gold. Unfortunately, it's not that simple.

But there is a real purpose in living a Jewish life. But that purpose is not found in some amorphous or self-defined concept of spirituality. That purpose is not to be found over the rainbow. And we are not for a moment to think we've found our purpose if we've been fortunate or lucky enough to have found our own pot of gold.

To put it simply, our purpose in life is in the way we live our lives. It's in navigating the journey we call life. It's in using our God given talents and abilities to do good for others and to bring others along on our journey. I'll let you in on a little secret. God has laid out this journey for us.

I invite you to take this journey. Travel down this path. Don't worry, I've brought along a JPS - kind of like a GPS system, only for Jews, and I've consulted the Jewish Mapquest so that we don't get lost.

Before we set out on our journey, in fact before we set out on any journey, we must first recite the "Tefilat Haderech," the Traveler's Prayer. It's a prayer for a safe journey recited by us whenever we travel, whether by air, sea, and even long car trips. It's one of the most important prayers we have, especially when we're speaking of 'journey'.

"May it be Your will, our God and the God of our ancestors, that You lead us toward peace, guide our footsteps toward peace, and make us reach our desired destination for life, gladness, and peace. May You rescue us from the hand of every foe, and ambush along the way, and from all manner of punishments that assemble to come to earth. May You send blessing in our handiwork, and grant us grace, kindness, and mercy in Your eyes and in the eyes of all who see us. May You hear the sound of our humble request because You are God Who hears prayer requests. Blessed are You, Adonai, Who hears prayer."

Now that we have asked God for His blessing on our journey, let us begin. I've even hired a tour guide for this trip; a young woman who you are undoubtedly familiar with. In thinking about purpose and how many of us look over the rainbow, I thought of no one better to lead us than Dorothy Gale, a young lady from Kansas.

I don't know, I don't believe, I've never seen any proof, that L. Frank Baum, the author of the Wizard of Oz, was Jewish. But The Wizard of Oz just might be one of the most quintessentially Jewish stories ever written. So let's join Dorothy on her journey and see if we can make it our own.

Dorothy was a young girl living in a small farmhouse with her Auntie Em, Uncle Henry, and her dog Toto. She was surrounded by an extended family of farmhands who also loved her. But that wasn't enough. Dorothy longed for something more. Life in Kansas wasn't satisfactory. She had to search for her own spirituality, for her own place over the rainbow.

Dorothy's spiritual journey began in turmoil. She was uprooted from her home and transported to another land. A land that was strange and different. A land that was .....in Color! What happened in that land though is important. The people she met there were the ones who she learned the most from, both good and bad.

First Dorothy meets Glinda, the Good Witch; the Witch of the East. How coincidental that she's from the East, the direction we face when we pray; the direction of Jerusalem!

Who is Glinda? Glinda is the embodiment of those people in our lives who are always there for us, who guide us, who advise us, who love us unconditionally, right or wrong. Glinda represents our parents, or our grandparents; our closest family members; the ones who raised us, nurtured us, taught us. They, like Glinda, are always there guiding us, caring for us, protecting us, even if we don't always realize it. We need people like that in our lives We are blessed to have them and should be grateful and appreciative for them. Perhaps one of our purposes in life is to learn to appreciate more the Glindas in our lives.

Then we meet the munchkins. As we journey through life we meet many munchkins. They are small, not necessarily so much in stature, but small in the sense of the role they play in our lives. They come and they go. They aren't always there for us. Some of them really are small people, both literally and figuratively. Our task is to block out their figurative smallness.

Many of these munchkins can and do help us. They point us in the right direction. They give us sage advice, and maybe we never see them again. But they served their purpose and we should be thankful. In our journey, what was their purpose? They pointed us on our path. They told us to follow the "Yellow Brick Road."

The Yellow Brick Road is the true path of life which leads to our destination. But like the road of life, the Yellow Brick Road is not paved with gold. It's paved with bricks. As we know, bricks can be used to build, or they can be used to destroy. It is therefore up to us, as we travel down this Yellow Brick Road, to decide how we use those bricks. Do we use them to build? Or do we use them to destroy?

We've already met the munchkins, the small people in our lives, and we've met the Glindas, the most important people in our lives. But there are so many more people who we meet on this journey, people who not only help us find our purpose, but hopefully help to make us more human. We do this by meeting people who have those traits, those values, that perhaps we are lacking or haven't yet developed.

The opposite is also true. We also encounter people who are missing those important traits, and their failings impact us and cause us to fail and fall. As much as we are trying to be fully human, we meet people who lack those elements which make them fully human. This is why, as we journey down the Yellow Brick Road of life, we meet people who lack intelligence, who don't have hearts, and who don't have any courage.

As Dorothy later learns, maybe we misjudged these people. Maybe the people that we thought had no brain, Scarecrows, if you will, who we thought could never offer us advice or help, in reality do. And so, we must give that person a second and even a third chance to show us what they really are about. To show us that we can learn from them just as they can learn from us.

Part of our purpose in life is to impart to those who have no brain, figuratively speaking, the benefit of ours. We need to share our wisdom with them, to offer them good advice and counsel, and to help steer them on the proper path. We also encounter people who do have a brain; who do give us sage advice; who do help us find our purpose in life. Our task is to search these people out, to listen to them and to take them along with us on our journey.

Similarly, we meet people who don't have a heart. Tin Men. Unfortunately we meet a lot of them in our lifetime. Our purpose is to transform them, to give them a heart by sharing ours. Our purpose is to show them the values of compassion and caring. We can do that. Perhaps this is our greatest purpose in life.

Again, the opposite is also true. We meet plenty of people who do have hearts, big ones at that. And they teach us how to have big hearts. They share with us; they help us; they don't put themselves first. They put others first. They do mitzvot for others. We can and must learn from them and emulate them as well.

We next meet people who have no courage; Cowardly Lions. These are people who have no faith, and no strength of their convictions. They are perfectly satisfied to just go along in life and not make waves. Our purpose is to get them involved, to support the causes and ideals that we as Jews believe in and care about, like Synagogues and Israel. We can do this, but only if we ourselves have the courage to do so. Perhaps our purpose is to show others the courage of our convictions by getting them to join with us in our journey; by getting them to believe or to be involved in what is truly important.

Then we meet those who do have courage; who teach us to stand up for ourselves and for what we believe; to stand up to evil and anti-Semitism wherever it may be found. These are people who we know will stand up for us. It is most important that we take them along with us on our journey. Their courage, their bravery, is an example that we should emulate.

Next we encounter the Wicked Witch. The Wicked Witch is the person or persons who try to sabotage our purpose, who try with all their might to knock us off our path. We might call it the yetzer hara, the evil inclination, or Satan, or even the devil. They use everything at their disposal to corrupt us. They use poppy fields and flying monkeys. They entice us with a pot of gold, with an easy way of life, with assimilation and with unfulfilled promises. Unfortunately, far too many of us are easily seduced by this.

This is why, in order to truly succeed in achieving our purpose, we must begin by ridding ourselves of the Wicked Witches in our lives. If nothing else, if we do that, our lives will be much happier and we will all be much better people for it.

If we've made it past the Wicked Witch, if we've doused her with a bucket of water and retrieved her broomstick, if we've taken the people who have a brain, a heart and courage with us on our journey, where exactly are we in this journey?

At the end of the Yellow Brick Road is the Emerald City. In the Emerald City there is a palace. In that palace is a large hallway and at the end of that large hallway is a curtain. Behind that curtain .... is a Wizard.

A Wizard. Who is that Wizard and what does he represent? Most spiritual seekers would naturally say that the Wizard is God. But we know that the Wizard was really a sham. He had no magic powers. He was a mere mortal.

And so at the end of our long journey we leave disappointed. We might have been looking for a Wizard, but we came to realize that the Wizard isn't really all that powerful. We realized that there really is no magic, no spell, no potion, no secret formula, that will get us where we need to be. So we are tempted to say, what was the point; what was the purpose of this journey?

The purpose, is that the path itself, whether we call it Halacha or the Yellow Brick Road, is important; not so much what we find at the end. It's what we encounter on that path - the people that we meet along the way – who stay with us, who impact us, and who affect us.

In Judaism, this path should lead us to the synagogue, to the Ark, and ultimately to the Torah. But the Torah isn't a Wizard either. It isn't magic. Even the Torah is not going to miraculously solve all our problems. But like the Wizard, it can dispense a lot of good advice.

It is why the words of the Shema resonate so clearly. The Shema prayer tells us to use our heart, to use our soul, and to use our might - to get there - not only to God, but to reach others as well.

At the end of The Wizard of Oz, what does Dorothy ultimately learn? "There's no place like home!" The people at home who love us the most, our families and our extended families, our friends and neighbors, are what really matters in life. Dorothy learns, as should we, that the journey we share with them is what counts.

We must not run away and hide from this purpose, and we must not search for it in far off places. Rather, we must realize and appreciate that we can find our purpose right here; right where we are. In our own homes and communities.

All we need to do is follow the path which God has laid out for us; not the Yellow Brick Road, but the Blue and White Road; a road paved with Jewish history, tradition, and values. Judaism has given us this path, a rather wide one, capable of encompassing a variety of Jewish practices and ideals, as well as a tour guide; the Torah. If we follow this Blue and White Road, if we stay on this path, we know we are heading in the right direction. All we need to do is embrace our Jewish heritage, our Jewish identities, and our Jewish community at large. All we need to do is follow this path in order to live a more fulfilling Jewish life. And all we need to do is act with intelligence, heart and courage, with all those whom we meet along the way on that Blue and White Road.

IN CONCLUSION
MAY THE LORD

God tells Moses to "Speak to Aaron and his sons: Thus shall you bless the people of Israel. Say to them, Yevarechecha Adonai Vyishmerecha;
Yaer Adonai Panav Eylecha Vyechuneka;
Yisa Adonai Panav Elecha V'yasem Lecha Shalom."
We know this more familiarly as,
May the Lord Bless you and keep you;
May the Lord show you favor and be gracious to you;
May the Lord show you kindness and grand you peace.
We know this blessing well. It is a blessing which is not only reserved for the priests, for the Kohens, but is also how we bless our children, bless a bar or bat mitzvah child, and bless a wedding couple. In other words, this is THE blessing which Jews bestow upon other Jews.

There are however two aspects of this blessing with which I wish to conclude this book.

The first is How this blessing should be delivered. The Talmud tells us the blessing which is recited before the

301

Kohanim bless us with the priestly blessing itself. This blessing reads, "Who commanded us to bless His people Israel with love."

With love! In order for it to truly be a blessing it must be heartfelt; it must be sincere; it must be delivered with love.

The second aspect involves the translation of the second blessing, "May the Lord show you favor and be gracious to you." That last word, in Hebrew, "v'yechuneka," is usually and correctly translated as being gracious. Nevertheless, it reminds me of the word "Chinuch," meaning education or learning. And that word reminds me of dedication, as in the holiday of Hanukkah.

This blessing should not only be delivered with love, but it should be bestowed on those who have dedicated and committed themselves to a Jewish way of life, Jews like the great sage Hillel, whose interpretation of Judaism was based on love for and dedication and commitment to, his fellow Jew and to the growth of the Jewish religion.

This is how we must act today, by emulating not just Hillel, but all those who follow his ways. By showing commitment and dedication to the Jewish people and to the Jewish religion, each of us are worthy recipients of that priestly blessing in its entirety.

I trust that these pages have given you some food for thought, have increased your knowledge of Judaism in some small way, and most importantly, have encouraged you to become more engaged and connected with your Jewish heritage.

And so I don't say to you, "MAY the Lord," because that is not what the blessing says.

Rather I say to you, with love and with dedication, knowing that you will continue to follow this path,

"The Lord will bless you and protect you!

The Lord will deal kindly and graciously with you!

The Lord will bestow His favor upon you and grant you peace!"

Amen and Ken Yehi Ratzon!

Made in the USA
Middletown, DE
23 July 2018